Classic Recipes from Scotland

For J.E.B. 143

Classic Recipes
from Scotland

Tom Bridge

MAINSTREAM
PUBLISHING

EDINBURGH AND LONDON

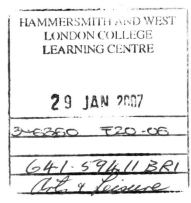
First published in Great Britain in 2005 by
MAINSTREAM PUBLISHING COMPANY
(EDINBURGH) LTD
7 Albany Street
Edinburgh EH1 3UG

ISBN 1 84018 943 6

A catalogue record for this book is available
from the British Library

Images © Mainstream, Tom Bridge, Donald Russell, Orkney Marketing Services, Jonathan
Lowry, De Vere Cameron House, Loch Fyne Oysters Ltd, The Edrington Group, Klinge Foods,
Jill Adron, Salar Smokehouse, Dickinson & Morris and www.istockphoto.com

Every effort has been made to trace all copyright holders. The publishers
will be glad to make good any omissions brought to their attention

Typeset in Apollo and Gill

Printed by Appl, Germany

contents

introduction

It was in the late 1960s, during my days training as a chef, that I discovered Scotland. On an exchange with other students, I travelled to Oban, then the Isle of Mull and finally on to Lagavulin Bay on the south side of Islay. I was born in Bolton, a northern mill town, and the first thing I noticed was how varied and beautiful the landscape was; it was to me the most picturesque place I had ever seen. The quality and freshness of the food I tasted on that trip made an enormous impression on me – I returned home telling my friends that they had never tasted beef until they had tasted Aberdeen Angus. This first visit sparked a lifelong passion for Scottish food and drink.

After I had completed my training and spent time working in hotel kitchens in London and the north of England, I decided to work for myself on a freelance basis. During the 1970s there were some definite advantages to this approach, as if I did not like the kitchen or area I was working in, I would call my agent, Sonia Cohen, to pull me out and find me a new job elsewhere.

At one point when I was freelancing for a Manchester catering agency, Sonia asked me if I would like to go to Scotland for a few months. After the happy experience of my previous visit, I jumped at the chance.

My first appointment in Scotland was an excellent choice by Sonia. I went to work for a truly old-fashioned lady called Ma Burns – tweed suits and all that – who owned the Pickwick Hotel on Racecourse Road in Ayr, near the beach and esplanade. She was a very proud woman who doted on her eighteenth-century three-star hotel and restaurant, and I was astonished when I was given a free hand to do what I liked with the menu for the Pickwick's restaurant. At that stage of my life, I was an avid reader of old cookery books and before I took a position, I would read up on the style of food the restaurant specialised in. So, with my 25-shilling volume of Marian F. McNeill's *The Scots Kitchen*, I went into a week's hibernation reading about Scottish food. Ma Burns and I had a wonderful time researching and working on traditional Scottish recipes. I was booked for just one month but I stayed for eighteen. I enjoyed my experience tremendously and it deepened my love of Scottish cuisine.

The difference in making soup alone was a joy. The water in the south of England is hard and tasteless but the waters of Scotland are soft, making them excellent for stocks and soups. Meanwhile, my knowledge of Scotland, its food and its people was beginning to build. My time off was always spent touring the country, enjoying the food and drink in restaurants around Scotland and finding out about its history.

In the years following my time in Ayr, I travelled around Scotland on several occasions, made many friends and worked with chefs from Gretna to Wick. Then, in 1996, when I was writing my book *Bridge over Britain*, I was given the opportunity of touring Britain with one of the country's best food photographers, David George. The two months we spent in Scotland were the highlight of the trip for me and left me with the fondest of memories.

You will be able to tell from my book that I have a great passion for food and for enjoying the finer things in life, sometimes to the extreme. However, just over three years ago, I had a wake-up call. Over a number of years, I had suffered from high blood pressure and I took medication for this. I had been feeling tired for a few weeks but put this down to overwork and running around too much on various projects. Finally, however, I had a brain haemorrhage and without the skill and dedication of Dr Tim Pigott and the neurosurgery team at the Walton Centre in Liverpool, I would not have been given my second chance in life.

Recuperation has been a long road and I know there were times when without the love of my wife, Jayne, and my boys I might well have given up. During this period, I had to take one step forward and then two back. As I came through the surgery, they found I had lost my sight. But for the dedication of my two eye surgeons, I would still be blind today.

So how did this bring me to my new adventure in Scotland? This came about because Jayne had heard me talking about my love of Scotland in the past and her close friend Gaynor had told her about the stunning scenery of Loch Lomond and the tranquillity of Cameron House Hotel on its banks. It seemed to her that a trip there might be just the thing to aid my recuperation.

Our weekend was booked and everything arranged. Because of my health problems, I was a little concerned as to how I would react to the journey and I was

still having headaches as a result of the haemorrhage. However, the minute we drove through the gates at Cameron House, I was met with a vision of perfect beauty and all worries were soon forgotten. After enjoying some of the most exquisite food and service I have ever encountered, in the Georgian Room restaurant, we decided to extend our stay. Jayne and I knew that I had been given a second chance at life and one of the things I decided then was that Scotland would become an integral part of my life. We were fortunate enough to purchase a lodge at Cameron House under the De Vere Resort Ownership scheme.

My next aspiration at this time was to be able to write another book – and it had to be on Scottish food. This has been one of the most difficult challenges I have ever taken on: with the problems with my sight, it has taken me nearly two years to complete but because of the experiences I have had and the wonderful people I have met while touring Scotland, what could have been a struggle became more and more of a pleasure.

Over the last three years, we have managed to visit Scotland on a regular basis as part of my research, giving me the opportunity to taste the nation's outstanding food and to don my cookery detective hat, touring the Highlands, writing for magazines and newspapers, demonstrating for television and talking on radio shows about food, which, I am sure you have gathered, is my favourite subject.

Eating in numerous hotels, restaurants and inns during this time, I gained an insight into the thriving Scottish gastronomic scene. This book is therefore a collection of recipes not only for great traditional dishes but also for the kind of modern-day classics that feature on the menus of restaurants and gastropubs throughout Scotland and which I am sure you will enjoy making for friends and family.

Each chapter focuses on a particular ingredient, such as fish or game, or type of cooking, like baking or jam-making, with a little history of Scottish fare added to the mix – and there are details of how to hold a Burns Supper, so that you can bring friends together for a celebratory evening of Scottish food and drink wherever you are in the world.

Of course, what makes Scottish cuisine truly great is the abundance of wonderful natural produce: the moors and forests filled with game; the Highlands, where the finest beef in the world is raised; and the lochs and rivers which support salmon, trout, mussels and oysters. Scotland is also rich in farmers and artisanal producers who use traditional methods to create truly wonderful products. It is for this reason that, with the help of the Scottish Food Information Executive, I have compiled a list of recommended suppliers with mail-order contact details to enable you to use the best authentic ingredients no matter how far you are from Scotland.

I have been involved with the food of Great Britain nearly all my life and in recent years I have frequently been asked by television producers and food manufacturers to re-create old recipes or invent new ones to take account of the trend towards healthy eating. Because of these concerns, you can use low-fat alternatives for any of the recipes throughout this cookbook in place of the butter, full-fat milk and cream mentioned in the various chapters.

I would also recommend that whenever salt is called for you use LoSalt. This is nothing to do with LoSalt being a Scottish company (although it is) but because it is far better for you. Medical evidence suggests that excessive sodium salt in the diet may aggravate high blood pressure. LoSalt is high in natural potassium and low in sodium salt, so for the health-conscious person, it is now possible to season food as usual while reducing sodium intake.

Anyone who thinks there is little more to Scottish cooking than haggis, porridge and shortbread has only to glance through these pages to see that there are many truly wonderful Scottish recipes to enjoy.

Happy cooking,
TTB

conversion tables

In the recipes, quantities are given in metric and imperial, and temperatures in Centigrade, Fahrenheit and Gas Mark. Tablespoons and teaspoons are also used, these being measurements of 15 ml and 5 ml respectively.

WEIGHTS		MEASURES		TEMPERATURES		
				Centigrade	Fahrenheit	Gas Mark
1 oz	28 g	2 fl. oz	60 ml	140	275	1
2 oz	56 g	3 fl. oz	90 ml	150	300	2
3 oz	84 g	¼ pt	150 ml	160	325	3
4 oz	112 g	½ pt	300 ml	180	350	4
5 oz	140 g	¾ pt	450 ml	190	375	5
6 oz	168 g	1 pt	600 ml	200	400	6
7 oz	196 g	1 ¼ pt	750 ml	210	415	7
8 oz	224 g	1 ¾ pt	1 litre	220	425	8
9 oz	252 g	2 pt	1.25 litres	240	450	9
10 oz	280 g	2 ½ pt	1.5 litres			
11 oz	308 g	3 ½ pt	2 litres			
12 oz	336 g					
13 oz	364 g					
14 oz	392 g					
15 oz	420 g					
1 lb	448 g					
1 ¼ lb	560 g					
1 ½ lb	672 g					
1 ¾ lb	784 g					
2 lb	896 g					
3 lb	1 kg 344 g					
4 lb	1 kg 792 g					
5 lb	2 kg 240 g					

stocks, sauces and soups

The great chefs and cooks of the British Isles all have one thing in common: they never throw away the water in which meat, fish or vegetables have been boiled. This is the basis for good stock for soups and sauces.

Soup has always been part of the Scottish diet – the Scots have to be the soup-lovers of the world. With hundreds of recipes at hand, I have picked the favourites from around the coastlines, towns and villages of Scotland.

I would like to dedicate this chapter to John Cumming, managing director of Loch Ness Mountain Spring Water, and chef Robert McKim at the Machrie Hotel (see Cock-a-Leekie soup on p. 33).

All the stock recipes here will make somewhat more than 600 ml/1 pt.

beef stock

900 g/2 lb beef bones
450 g/1 lb shin of Scottish beef
50 g/2 oz dripping
2 leeks
1 large onion
1 stick of celery
2 large carrots
2 bouquets garnis
4 white peppercorns
4 tbsp white wine vinegar
1 sprig of thyme
salt
freshly milled black pepper

Preheat the oven to 220°C/425°F/Gas Mark 8.

Blanch the bones for 10 minutes in boiling water. Cut up the shin of beef and put it with the bones and the dripping in a large roasting tin. Roast in the centre of the oven for 40 minutes.

Put the bones and meat in a large deep casserole or pan. Add the cleaned, roughly chopped vegetables and all the other ingredients. Cover with cold water and bring the contents slowly to the boil, remove any scum from the surface and cover the casserole or pan with a tight-fitting lid.

Simmer the stock over the lowest heat for 3 hours to extract all the flavour from the bones and vegetables, topping up with hot water if the level of stock should fall below the ingredients.

Strain the stock through a fine sieve into a large bowl. Leave it to settle for 5 minutes and then remove the fat from the surface by drawing absorbent kitchen paper over it.

chicken stock

4 tbsp cooking oil
350 g/12 oz chicken giblets, chopped
1.5 kg/3 lb boiling chicken, jointed
2 leeks, trimmed
1 large onion
1 stick celery
2 large carrots
2 bouquets garnis
4 white peppercorns
8 juniper berries
4 tbsp white wine vinegar
1 litre/1¾ pt cold water
1 sprig thyme
salt
freshly milled black pepper

Heat the oil in a large saucepan. Clean and roughly chop the vegetables. Add the giblets and chicken to the oil with the leeks, onion, celery and carrots, and cook for 10 minutes.

Add the rest of the ingredients to the pan and bring the contents slowly to the boil. Remove any scum from the surface and cover the saucepan with a tight-fitting lid.

Simmer the stock over a low heat for 90 minutes to extract all the flavour from the giblets and vegetables.

Top up with hot water if the liquid should fall below the level of the ingredients.

Strain the stock through a fine sieve into a large bowl. Leave the stock to settle for 5 minutes, then remove the fat from the surface by drawing absorbent kitchen paper over it.

game stock

You can use any game bones you like here, including venison, guinea fowl, quail, hare and rabbit.

900 g/2 lb game bones
450 g/1 lb shin of Scottish beef
50 g/2 oz dripping
2 leeks
1 large onion
1 stick of celery
2 large carrots
2 bouquets garnis
6 juniper berries
4 white peppercorns
4 tbsp red wine vinegar
1 sprig of thyme
1 sprig of rosemary
salt
freshly milled black pepper

Preheat the oven to 220°C/425°F/Gas Mark 8.

Blanch the bones for 10 minutes in boiling water. Cut up the shin of beef and put it with the bones and the dripping in a large roasting tin. Roast in the centre of the oven for 40 minutes.

Put the bones and meat in a large deep casserole or pan. Clean and roughly chop the vegetables and add them to the pan with all the other ingredients. Cover with cold water and bring the contents slowly to the boil, remove any scum from the surface and cover the casserole or pan with a tight-fitting lid.

Simmer the stock over the lowest heat for 3 hours to extract all the flavour from the bones and vegetables, topping up with hot water if the level of stock should fall below the ingredients.

Strain the stock through a fine sieve into a large bowl. Leave it to settle for 5 minutes and then remove the fat from the surface by drawing absorbent kitchen paper over it.

giblet stock

50 g/2 oz duck fat
450 g/1 lb mixed chicken and turkey giblets
2 leeks
1 large onion
1 stick of celery
2 large carrots
2 bouquets garnis
4 white peppercorns
8 juniper berries
4 tbsp white wine vinegar
1 litre/1¾ pt chicken stock
1 sprig of thyme
salt
freshly milled black pepper

Heat the duck fat in a large saucepan, chop the giblets and add them to the duck fat with the cleaned and roughly chopped leeks, onion, celery and carrots, and cook for 10 minutes.

Add the rest of the ingredients and bring the contents slowly to the boil, remove any scum from the surface and cover the saucepan with a tight-fitting lid.

Simmer the stock over a low heat for 90 minutes to extract all the flavour from the giblets and vegetables.

If the liquid reduces until it no longer covers the ingredients, top it up with hot water.

Strain the stock through a fine sieve into a large bowl. Leave it to settle for 5 minutes and then remove the fat from the surface by drawing absorbent kitchen paper over it.

vegetable stock

For vegetable stock, it is very important that you use large pieces of fresh, clean vegetables. Do not use cabbage, cauliflower or sprouts, as they have a very distinctive taste and smell, and will dominate the stock.

  2 carrots, peeled and sliced
  2 leeks, trimmed
  2 onions, sliced
  1 swede, peeled and diced
  12 shallots, unpeeled
  1 large parsnip, peeled and sliced
  8 sticks celery, sliced
  2 litres/3½ pt water
  4 tbsp white wine vinegar
  salt
  freshly milled black pepper
  sprig of thyme
  sprig of parsley

Put all the ingredients in a large saucepan and simmer for 1 hour.
    Pass through a fine sieve, cool and store until required.

fish stock

When cooking fish, do not throw away the heads, skins and trimmings as they can be used to make stock. Make use of the bones from monkfish, turbot, whiting and sole. Cheap white fish can also be used but do not use oily fish such as mackerel or herring. You can also ask your fishmonger for bones, heads and broken fish. Fish stock should be used within 48 hours but it freezes well.

1.8 kg/4 lb fish bones and trimmings
50 g/2 oz butter
200 g/8 oz onion, finely chopped
200 g/8 oz leek, finely chopped
200 g/8 oz celery, finely chopped
juice of 1 lemon
8 peppercorns
1 bay leaf
sprig of parsley
150 ml/⅓ pt white wine
4 tbsp white wine vinegar
2 litres/3½ pt water

Thoroughly wash the fish bones and roughly chop them up.

Melt the butter in a large pan. Cook the vegetables for 3 minutes until they are slightly soft. Add the bones and the remainder of the ingredients except the water. Cook for 8 minutes until the wine is slightly reduced. Add the water, bring to the boil, skim off any froth which has risen to the surface and then simmer for 30 minutes.

Pass the stock through a sieve and allow it to cool, leaving it to stand for 1 hour.

court bouillon

This is a basic stock in which to poach fish.

Poaching any fish, especially wild salmon, in court bouillon will give it a unique flavour.

2 litres/3½ pt water
600 ml/1 pt dry white wine
100 g/4 oz carrots, finely chopped
100 g/4 oz leek, finely chopped
100 g/4 oz onion or shallots, finely chopped
1 stick of celery, finely chopped
1 sprig each of dill, thyme and rosemary
1 clove of garlic
1 bay leaf
8 white peppercorns
4 tbsp white wine vinegar
4 coriander seeds

In a very large pan, bring the water and white wine to the boil. Add all the ingredients and allow the stock to simmer for 15 minutes.

Let the stock stand for at least 2 hours before you poach any fish in it. This will enhance the flavour of the fish you are to poach.

After it's been used to cook fish, the court bouillon can be frozen in small quantities in freezer bags and used when you need fish stock.

espagnole sauce

This is without doubt one of the great classics in both British and French cuisine and it is very important to chefs of both nationalities, for it is the base for many sauces – without this brown sauce, perfect gravy could never have been made. The great chefs of the two countries agree that short cuts must be avoided when making sauces.

Makes 600 ml/1 pt

50 g/2 oz butter
50 g/2 oz plain flour
1 litre/1¾ pt beef stock
2 tbsp white wine vinegar
1 heaped tbsp tomato purée

FOR THE MIREPOIX:
100 g/4 oz bacon, finely diced
100 g/4 oz carrots, finely diced
100 g/4 oz onion, finely diced
50 g/2 oz celery, finely diced
50 g/2 oz leek, finely diced
50 g/2 oz fresh fennel, finely diced
1 sprig thyme
1 small bay leaf
salt
freshly milled black pepper

First, make a roux: melt the butter in a saucepan and stir in the flour. Cook over a low heat, stirring occasionally to prevent the mixture from browning. After about three minutes, when it has coloured slightly and thickened, take the pan off the heat.

Meanwhile, bring the stock to the boil. Add the tomato purée to the roux; slowly add the boiling stock and vinegar, and blend thoroughly with a plastic-coated balloon whisk or a wooden spoon.

Make the mirepoix by sautéing the vegetables and bacon with a little oil or butter until the mixture is a soft golden colour.

Drain the vegetables of the liquid they have produced, add this to the sauce with the herbs and seasoning, and discard the vegetables. Simmer slowly for at least 4 hours. The sauce should have the consistency of single cream. If you need to thin it, add a little water or stock. Skim and then strain through a fine sieve into a clean saucepan.

pepper sauce

For a simple pepper sauce for steak, add 1 tablespoon of green peppercorns with some freshly milled black pepper and 2 tablespoons of double cream to 150 ml/$\frac{1}{4}$ pt of espagnole sauce.

demi-glace sauce

To make a demi-glace sauce, just add 1 litre/$1\frac{3}{4}$ pint of espagnole sauce to 1 litre/$1\frac{3}{4}$ pt of beef stock, cook for 10 minutes, correct the seasoning, then put through a fine sieve.

This can be used to make gravies or wine sauces. It freezes well.

onion gravy

One of the finest British cooks I ever met was Francis Coulson, who, with Brian Sack, owned one of the first and finest country-house hotels in Britain, Sharrow Bay in the Lake District. Francis is sadly is no longer with us. He would always say to me during our talks about sauces, 'Never decry the word gravy,' and he is so right. The flavour of gravy is one of the most wonderful tastes in British cookery. He would then repeat the saying, adding: 'It will not be proper gravy if you use a beef stock cube, the flavour will be far superior if you use a traditional beef stock recipe.'

50 g/2 oz dripping
4 rashers of naturally cured rindless Ayrshire back bacon, finely chopped
3 large red onions, peeled and sliced
2 tbsp dry sherry
60 m/2 fl. oz red wine vinegar
50 g/2 oz plain flour
600 ml/1 pt of fresh beef stock (see p. 14)
bouquet garni
2 tsp tomato purée
2 tsp Worcestershire sauce
salt
freshly milled black pepper

Melt the dripping in a heavy-based pan; add the bacon and onions, cooking for 6 minutes until the onions are light brown. Add the sherry and vinegar, and cook for 3 minutes.

Blend in the flour, stirring the roux until it is brown. Gradually add half the beef stock, stirring constantly until the mixture has cooked through and thickened. Add the bouquet garni and simmer for 30 minutes. Add the tomato paste, Worcestershire sauce, seasoning and beef stock, simmering and skimming for a further 30 minutes. Keep checking the seasoning all the time.

Strain through a fine sieve and skim off any extra fat.

When I am serving onion gravy for Yorkshire puddings, I always add the juice from the roast beef to the above with an extra finely chopped onion.

madeira sauce

This is great with steak or roast beef, and I particularly recommend it with my Scotch beef with puff pastry (see p. 90).

275 ml/½ pt Madeira
4 tbsp port
75 g/3 oz shallots, finely chopped
1 bay leaf
1 sprig thyme
pinch coarse-ground black peppercorns
250 ml/½ pt demi-glace sauce
salt
freshly milled black pepper

Put all the ingredients except the last three in a saucepan. Bring to the boil and allow to reduce by at least a quarter. Add the demi-glace sauce and simmer for 15 minutes. Season with salt and pepper, and strain through a fine sieve.

arran mustard and whisky sauce

I recommend this sauce with black pudding (see p. 61) but it is also excellent with chicken and pork. I suggest using an 8-year-old Macallan Fine Oak.

    1 large red onion, finely chopped
    50 g/2 oz butter
    2 tbsp plain flour
    3 tbsp wine vinegar
    100 ml/3 fl. oz beef stock (see p. 14)
    zest and juice of 1 orange
    zest and juice of 1 lemon
    4 tbsp redcurrant jelly
    4 tbsp Arran mustard
    60 ml/2 fl. oz single-malt whisky
    pinch cayenne pepper
    salt
    freshly milled black pepper

Gently fry the chopped onion in the butter until soft, add the flour and cook for 2 minutes. Slowly add the wine vinegar, beef stock, and orange and lemon zest and juice, and simmer for a further 8 minutes. Add the rest of the ingredients and blend thoroughly. Cook for another 4 minutes.

chicken or game consommé

Serves 8–10

1.75 litres/3 pt chicken or game stock (see pp. 15–16)
150 ml/⅓ pt medium sherry
whites of 4 free-range eggs plus shells
salt
freshly milled black pepper
100 g/4 oz cooked corn-fed chicken breast or game meat

In a large saucepan, heat the chicken stock and sherry gently for 5 minutes.

Add the egg whites and shells to the chicken stock and whisk until the mixture begins to boil. When the liquid boils, remove the pan from the heat and allow the mixture to subside for 10 minutes before skimming. Repeat this process 3 times. This allows the egg white to trap the sediments in the chicken stock, clarifying the soup.

Let the consommé cool for 5 minutes.

Carefully place a piece of fine muslin over a clean saucepan and strain the soup into the saucepan. Repeat this process twice, then gently reheat the consommé, season, taste and place to one side. Place the hot, thinly sliced cooked chicken or game meat into a warm soup tureen, pour over the consommé and serve immediately.

THE PRINCE AND THE BREE

Hotchpotch, known also as hairst bree (harvest broth), was made only when the kailyard, or kitchen garden, was in its prime. It is related that Prince Albert, when on board a Highland loch steamer, was lured to the galley by the delicious odour of hotchpotch.

'How is it made?' he asked the cook, who failed to recognise him.

'Weel, there's mutton intill't and neeps intill't and peas intill't—'

'But what's "intill't?"' asked the prince.

'I'm telling ye, there's mutton intill't and neeps intill't and—'

'Yes, but what's "intill't?"'

'Gudesake, man, am I no thrang tellin' ye what's intill't?! There's mutton intill't . . .'

The timely arrival of a member of the Prince's suite put an end to the confusion. He explained that 'intill't' meant 'into it' and nothing more.

hotchpotch

For a really wholesome flavour, use 50 per cent beef stock and 50 per cent chicken stock. I recommend using organic lamb for this recipe. One of the finest producers is Liz Ramsay at Scottish Organic Lamb at Castle Douglas, Dumfries & Galloway. You can find Liz in the Recommended Suppliers section at the back of the book.

Serves 4

900 g/2 lb neck of lamb
1 litre/1¾ pt beef stock (see p. 14)
1 litre/1¾ pt chicken stock (see p. 15)
50 g/2 oz dripping
12 large spring onions, chopped
450 g/1 lb potatoes, peeled and sliced
2 carrots, peeled and sliced
225 g/8 oz peas, shelled
225 g/8 oz turnip, diced
225 g/8 oz fresh broad beans
1 medium cauliflower, cut into florets
1 tsp sugar or honey
2 tbsp chopped mint
salt
freshly milled black pepper
freshly chopped parsley

Remove the fat from the lamb and cut the meat into cubes. Soak the lamb in the beef and chicken stock for 2 hours. Melt the beef dripping in a large saucepan. Drain the lamb, reserving the stock, and brown for 5 minutes.

Pour in enough of the stock to just cover the lamb and simmer for 1 hour. Remove any scum from the top of the pan. Add the spring onions, potatoes, carrots, peas, turnip and broad beans, adding a little more stock. Cover and simmer for a further hour. Then add the cauliflower, sugar, mint and seasoning. Bring the soup to the boil and then simmer with a lid on the saucepan for 30 minutes, topping up with stock when required. Check the seasoning and sprinkle with freshly chopped parsley.

lorraine soup

This soup was named after Mary of Lorraine, mother of Mary Queen of Scots, who introduced the soup whilst on one of her many visits to Holyrood Palace in Edinburgh. This is usually served at traditional Scottish banquets during the festive season.

Serves 4

25 g/1 oz butter
25 g/1 oz flour
1 litre/1¾ pt chicken stock (see p. 15)
100 g/4 oz cooked chicken breast meat, finely chopped
zest of 1 lemon
⅓ tsp freshly grated nutmeg
150 ml/⅓ pt double cream
25 g/1 oz crushed almonds
salt
freshly milled white pepper
2 yolks of hard-boiled free-range egg, chopped

Heat the butter gently in a saucepan, add the flour and cook for 2 minutes. Slowly add the chicken stock and cook for 12 minutes on a low heat, stirring all the time.

Add the finely chopped chicken meat, lemon zest and nutmeg, cook for a further 12 minutes on a low heat. Stir in the cream, almonds, salt and pepper, simmer for 4 minutes and serve garnished with the chopped egg yolks.

mussel brose

The mussels at Loch Fyne are grown on ropes suspended from buoys. The mussels stay above the seabed and so are free of grit and beyond the reach of starfish, crabs and other denizens of the deep! For a modern-day mussel brose, substitute for the water half fish stock and half white wine to which 3 cloves of roughly chopped garlic have been added and use 50:50 milk and cream instead of milk.

Serves 4

1 kg/2 lb mussels
water
300 ml/½ pt milk
1 large onion, finely chopped
salt
freshly milled black pepper
30 g/1 oz oatmeal, toasted
150 ml/⅓ pt double cream

Wash the mussels under cold running water; discard any that do not close when tapped on a cutting board. Remove the beards and place the mussels in a large saucepan, just covering them with water. Gently bring to the boil and then simmer until all the shells are open, about 8 to 10 minutes.

Remove the mussels with a slotted spoon and place to one side to allow them to cool. Shell them, discarding any that have not opened, and strain the cooking liquid into a clean saucepan.

Add the milk and onion to the mussel liquid, heat gently, season well and then add the mussels, simmering for 10 minutes.

Put the oatmeal on a layer of cooking foil in the grill pan and brown under the grill. In a bowl, combine the toasted oats with about 300 ml/½ pt of the brose, blending quickly so that the mixture forms a dough which can be shaped into small dumplings.

Pour the soup into a tureen; add the cream and then the dumplings. Serve with doorstops of granary bread.

cream of lemon and lobster soup

The flavours of Victorian Scottish cookery come to the fore in this unusual recipe. During a stay over in the village of Cramond, I came across a variation using orange as well as lemon, and chicken rather than fish stock. I also tasted a delicious version of this soup at Gordon Ramsay's now sadly defunct Amaryllis restaurant in Glasgow.

Serves 4

50 g/2 oz butter
8 shallots, skinned and thinly sliced
2 medium-sized carrots, peeled and thinly sliced
2 stalks celery, washed and thinly sliced
450 g/1 lb fresh lobster meat, roughly chopped
zest and juice of 3 lemons

1.1 litres/2 pt fish stock (see p. 19)
salt
freshly ground white pepper
150 ml/¼ pt double cream
stalk of parsley
3 slices of lemon

Melt the butter in a large saucepan, add the vegetables and lobster meat, and cook gently for 5 minutes.

Grate the lemons and blanch the zest in boiling water for 3 minutes. Drain and add to the pan with the freshly squeezed lemon juice and the fish stock. Bring slowly to the boil and simmer for 30 minutes.

Cool the soup and put it through a blender.

Pour the soup back into the saucepan, reheat, season and add the double cream. *Do not boil* or the soup will curdle.

Pour the soup into a tureen or individual bowls and garnish with sprigs of parsley and half slices of lemon.

cullen skink

Cullen is a fishing village on the Moray Firth and skink means soup, stock or broth. This recipe traces its origins to the Moray Firth smokeries where oak chippings from old whisky barrels were first used in curing fish, adding the most unique flavour to finnan (smoked) haddock. Years ago, I created a recipe called Haddock Tam's Brig in a Taste of Scotland cookery competition in Ayrshire. Yes, I did win but I was given a tankard full of the taste of Scotland and cannot remember the rest of the evening or whatever happened to the tankard.

Serves 4

450 g/1 lb finnan haddock, skinned
600 ml/1 pt of fish stock (see p. 19)
600 ml/1 pt of milk
450 g/1 lb sliced potatoes, cooked
25 g/1 oz butter
salt
freshly milled black pepper

Place the haddock in a large saucepan, cover with boiling fish stock and simmer for about 6 minutes. Remove the fish from the stock and remove any bones from the fish.

Flake the haddock. Strain the stock, adding the milk, potatoes and flaked fish, and simmer for 20 minutes. Season and add the butter. You could also add a little cream if you like. Garnish with parsley and serve with crusty wholemeal bread.

For a more luxurious flavour, try this recipe with smoked salmon ends, which are far cheaper than the sides of smoked salmon, and top with flakes of uncooked smoked salmon. In this case, though, simmer the soup for only 10 minutes rather than 20.

loch fyne oyster soup

This soup is excellent cold in summer, topped with fresh strawberries and served with a dry white wine.

You can have seafood from Loch Fyne Oysters delivered to your door (see Recommended Suppliers).

Serves 4

24 fresh oysters
100 g/4 oz unsalted butter
50 g/2 oz plain white flour
1.2 litres/2 pt fish stock (see p. 19)
300 ml/½ pt cream
1 tbsp lemon juice
salt
freshly ground white pepper
2 free-range egg yolks
1 stalk of parsley, finely chopped

To open the oysters, wrap a napkin or tea towel around your (holding) hand. Place the oyster in the palm of your hand with the flat side facing upwards. Carefully slip an oyster knife, or a sharp kitchen knife solid enough not to bend, under the hinge in the shell and push it inside the shell; use the knife to lever the shell open.

Repeat this with all the oysters. Pour the juice from the oysters into a small jug and place the oysters in a bowl, ensuring that there are no bits of shell with them.

Heat the fish stock. Melt the butter in a large saucepan and blend in the flour. Add the fish stock, stirring continuously. Add the cream and lemon juice. Season with salt and white pepper.

Strain the soup through a fine non-metallic sieve into a clean saucepan; gently bring to the boil and immediately remove from the heat.

Just before you serve it, add the oysters, then blend the egg yolks with the oyster juice and whisk this mixture very carefully into the soup. Sprinkle with parsley and serve immediately.

machrie hotel cock-a-leekie

If you made this soup like chef Robert McKim at the Machrie Hotel on Islay, it could not be any purer. Why? Well, Robert buys his water from John Cumming at Loch Ness Mountain Spring Water in Inverness especially to make his soups and to wash his salads. If you are in the area, you must pay him a visit and taste this classic soup. This is really a main-course soup and was originally made with beef as well as chicken. Should you wish, you could put in a little rice and some diced red pepper at the same time as the prunes to add colour.

Serves 4

30 g/1 oz butter
350 g/12 oz uncooked chicken meat, cut into bitesize pieces
350 g/12 oz leeks, washed and cut into 2.5 cm/1 inch pieces
1 litre/1¾ pt chicken stock (see p. 15), made using natural spring water if possible
1 bouquet garni
salt
freshly ground white pepper
8 prunes, stoned and halved

Melt the butter in a large saucepan and fry the chicken and leeks for 8 minutes.
    Add the stock and bouquet garni, seasoning well to taste.
    Bring the soup to the boil and simmer for 45 minutes.
    Add the prunes and simmer for 20 minutes.

partan bree

This is a classic soup made from crabs, popular in all the coastal areas of Scotland.

I first tasted this at the Glen Mhor Hotel in Inverness, where I have been served some of the finest regional soups I ever tasted. The area is great for fishing, so your dinner is caught and landed straight into the pot! You can't get any fresher than that.

Serves 4

2 large cooked brown crabs
1.2 litres/2 pt chicken stock (see p. 15)
1 blade of mace
900 ml full-cream milk
75 g/3 oz long-grain white rice
150 ml/⅓ pt double cream
3 drops of anchovy essence
salt
freshly ground white pepper

Carefully remove all the meat from the crabs, discarding the feathery-looking gills and separating the white meat from the brown. Place the claw meat and the crab shells to one side.

Place the shells in a large pan with the chicken stock, add the blade of mace and simmer for 20 minutes.

Strain the liquid through a muslin-lined sieve into a clean saucepan.

Add the milk, rice and white crab meat, half the brown meat and any pink coral. Cover and simmer for 30 minutes.

Blend the soup in a liquidiser until smooth; add the rest of the crab meat, the cream and the anchovy essence. Reheat slowly – do not boil; season and taste, pour into a warm soup tureen and serve with warm, crusty wholemeal bread.

bawd bree, or scots hare soup

This recipe can also be made using rabbit. Should you not be fond of hare, you could substitute chicken and beef, for a version of the recipe which used to be called Cock and Bull.

Dr Alexander 'Jupiter' Carlyle, the popular minister of Inveresk in Midlothian who was a member of the circle of Enlightenment thinkers which included Adam Smith and David Hume, insisted on having currants in his hare soup, as was the fashion in the eighteenth century.

Serves 4

50 g/2 oz butter
1 small onion, peeled and diced
1 small carrot, peeled and diced
1 small turnip, peeled and diced
450 g/1 lb hare meat, diced
450 g/1 lb shin of beef, diced
50 g/2 oz plain flour
1 litre/1¾ pt game stock (see p. 16)
1 tbsp mushroom ketchup
1 bay leaf
6 black peppercorns
pinch salt
pinch cayenne pepper
3 tbsp redcurrant jelly
150 ml/⅓ pt port
50 g/2 oz oatmeal
25 g/1 oz currants (optional)

Melt the butter in a large saucepan, add the onions, carrot, turnip, hare and beef; cook slowly for 10 minutes and sprinkle with flour. Cook for a further 2 minutes and slowly add the stock with the mushroom ketchup, bay leaf, peppercorns, salt and cayenne pepper. Simmer for 2 hours.

Add the redcurrant jelly, port and oatmeal. Blend thoroughly and let the stock stand for at least 2 hours.

Remove the bay leaf and put the stock and meat through a blender or liquidiser.

Reheat and simmer for 25 minutes, serve with the currants, if liked, and crusty bread.

scotch broth

A firm family favourite, this really is a flavour of Scotland that will stay with you forever. The taste of organic mutton, barley, carrot, turnip, leeks and peas gives you the feeling of being in the glens watching the salmon jumping.

Serves 4

50 g/2 oz pre-soaked dried peas
900 g/2 lb neck of organic mutton, bones and fat removed, diced
1.2 litres/2 pt beef stock (see p. 14)
600 ml/1 pt water
50 g/2 oz barley, washed
salt
freshly ground white pepper
1 large carrot, peeled and diced
1 small turnip, peeled and diced
1 large leek, washed and cut thinly
1 red onion, finely chopped

Put the peas and mutton with the stock and water in a large pan. Bring slowly to the boil and skim the stock as it boils.

When all the scum is removed, add the washed barley and salt, and simmer for 25 minutes.

Add the rest of the ingredients and simmer for 2 hours and skim.

This soup improves with time and should be left for at least 24 hours and preferably 2 days to allow the flavours to develop, before being reheated and served with oatcakes (see p. 195) or bread.

game soup with sherry

This recipe is served in most game-shooting areas of Scotland and is very popular with the golfing fraternity, why I don't know. Maybe it has something to do with shooting a birdie!

Today, game can be bought in most large supermarkets and can also be purchased ready cut and trimmed.

For an extra boost to this recipe, replace half the beef stock with fresh unsweetened cranberry juice.

Serves 4

50 g/2 oz butter
1 onion, peeled and diced
1 carrot, peeled and diced
1 small turnip, peeled and diced
1 celery stick, diced
450 g/1 lb venison, fat removed, diced
450 g/1 lb game meat (e.g. rabbit, pheasant or grouse), chopped
50 g/2 oz plain flour
1 litre/1¾ pt beef stock (see p. 14)
1 tbsp mushroom ketchup
1 bay leaf
8 black peppercorns
pinch salt
3 tbsp redcurrant jelly
150 ml/⅓ pt of cream sherry

Melt the butter in a saucepan, add the onions, carrot, turnip, celery, venison and game meat, cook slowly for 6 minutes and then sprinkle with flour.

Cook for a further 2 minutes and slowly add the stock with the mushroom ketchup, bay leaf, peppercorns and salt. Simmer for 1 hour. Add the redcurrant jelly and sherry.

Leave to stand for at least 4 hours. Remove the bay leaf and put the soup through a blender or liquidiser.

Reheat and simmer for 10 minutes. Serve with croutons.

haggis and neep soup

A fellow chef, Steve Johnstone, gave me this recipe when he was head chef at Dalhousie Castle at Bonnyrigg near Edinburgh in 1996. It is basically a turnip soup, but flavoured with haggis, whisky and cream. The haggis already contains plenty of seasoning, so there is no need for extra salt and pepper.

Serves 4

50 g/2 oz butter
450 g/1 lb turnips, peeled and diced
1 large onion, chopped
2 large potatoes, peeled and chopped
1 tbsp chopped fresh parsley
1 litre/1¾ pt chicken stock
400 g haggis
60 ml/2 fl. oz single malt whisky
300 ml/½ pt double cream

In a large saucepan, melt the butter and add the turnip, onion and potato. Cook over a low heat for 10 minutes and add the parsley and chicken stock. Cover and simmer for 40 minutes until the vegetables are soft.

Add the haggis by crumbling it into the soup. Cook for 10 minutes, then put through a blender or liquidiser and purée until the soup has a smooth texture.

Return it to the pan; add the whisky and half the cream and very slowly heat through. Garnish with a swirl of cream and fresh nasturtium flowers. Serve with crusty brown bread and a glass of Orkney 18 Carat wine (see Orkney Wine Company in Recommended Suppliers).

savouries

To me, a savoury is the ultimate snack, brunch, lunch and supper dish. I love Arbroath smokies, black pudding, potted Orkney cheese, Scotch eggs made with Ayrshire pork sausage, and Scots toast – a sprinkling of all the best Scottish ingredients. If I were to open a restaurant, out of sheer laziness, I would call it Savouries; the menu would be on a large blackboard on the wall, made up of a selection of my favourite foods, which I know everyone would enjoy – a full Scottish breakfast at the forefront, followed by all the recipes in this chapter.

Most of the ingredients for these recipes can be found at the many Farmers' Markets around Scotland. Farmers' Markets are such good fun. You can have a tasting before you buy and it's a great way to meet new friends who enjoy food.

THE SCOTTISH BREAKFAST

A modern Highland breakfast is closely related to the meal of 200 years ago, with porridge with salt (no sugar), finnan haddie with poached eggs, Arbroath smokies, smoked salmon with scrambled eggs, potato scones, Ayrshire naturally cured bacon, mushrooms, girdle scones (thick pancakes), oatcakes, heather honey, gingerbread, Scots toast, butter and marmalade. A hundred years ago, this would also have included venison pasty, potted grouse, grilled trout and smoked mutton ham. See p. 162 for a traditional recipe for venison pasty.

porridge with whisky

My wife Jayne always starts her day with porridge and golden syrup. I like mine in the cold winter months with Macallan whisky. Every time I have friends or family over for a brunch, this gets everyone in a warm frame of mind. I first tasted this while visiting the Castle of Mey near John o' Groats, with its outstanding views north over the Pentland Firth and across to the Orkney Islands.

Many myths surround the making of porridge, so do beware when making it: some say it should be allowed to stand and then be reheated; others that it should be stirred in a clockwise direction using the right hand so you don't invoke the Devil; and others say it should be eaten standing up. I wonder what the three bears would have thought!

The top name in quality oats is Tilquhillie (see Recommended Suppliers), who produce 100 per cent natural oat products like the famous clootie dumpling. Porridge with whisky is also wonderful with heather honey drizzled over the top.

Serves 2

110 g/4 oz oat flakes
275 ml/9½ fl. oz water or milk
pinch salt
2 tbsp single malt whisky

Place the oats and water or milk in a small pan. Bring to the boil, stirring to encourage the porridge to thicken. When the porridge has thickened (about 5–7 minutes), remove from the heat. Add the salt and whisky before serving.

smoked salmon and scrambled eggs with orkney strubarb wine

The rich and famous today still demand this as a savoury starter during a Sunday brunch. A glass of crisp, fresh Orkney Strubarb, which is made with strawberries and Orkney-grown rhubarb, is the perfect complement to this dish.

Only the best Scottish smoked salmon should be used for this recipe and it should not be cooked with the scrambled egg – using that method only ruins the flavour of the smoked salmon.

Serves 4

225 g/8 oz Scottish smoked salmon, seasoned with black pepper
8 free-range eggs
5 tbsp double cream
salt
generous pinch freshly grated nutmeg
freshly milled black pepper
50 g/2 oz butter

Cut the sliced and seasoned smoked salmon into diamond shapes.

In a large bowl mix together the eggs, cream, salt, nutmeg and pepper, whisking them well.

Melt the butter slowly in a large non-stick frying pan, add the egg mixture and stir all the time using a wooden spoon until the mixture becomes creamy and is just thickening but not completely set.

Divide the scrambled eggs between warm plates and top with the diamonds of smoked salmon and serve with a chilled glass of Strubarb wine.

a fricassey of eggs

A fricassey, or fricassee, was in the sixteenth century a dish of various meats cooked together in a frying pan. By the eighteenth century, simpler versions involving rabbit or chicken in a creamy sauce were more common. This egg version is the logical conclusion of that trend towards cheaper, quicker dishes.

> Boil eight eggs hard, Take off the shells, cut them into quarters, have ready a half pint of Cream, and a quarter of a pound of fresh Butter, stir it together over the Fire till it is thick and smooth, lay the eggs in your dish and pour the same over. Garnish with the hard yolks of three eggs cut in two and lay around the edge of the dish.
> *The Art of Cookery Made Plain and Easy*, Mrs Hannah Glasse (1747)

kedgeree

Originally a spicy Indian recipe known as kitchri and containing onions and lentils, kedgeree was brought back to Britain for the breakfast table in the eighteenth century by the nabobs of the East India Company. It remains highly popular in the great Scottish hotels.

Serves 4

450 g/1 lb cooked finnan haddock, bones and skin removed
50 g/2 oz butter
pinch saffron powder
3 free-range eggs, hard-boiled and shelled
175 g/6 oz cooked long-grain rice
2 tbsp double cream
salt
freshly milled black pepper
fresh parsley or coriander, chopped

Flake the cooked finnan haddock, making sure all the bones and skin are removed.

Melt the butter in a medium saucepan; add the fish with a pinch of saffron. Chop the eggs and add them with the rice to the saucepan.

Gently heat all the ingredients together and slowly add the cream, stirring thoroughly. Season with salt and pepper and serve hot with a sprinkling of freshly chopped parsley or coriander leaves.

arbroath smokies

Arbroath smokies are young haddock that have been gutted and their heads removed; they then undergo a long smoking process until they are a dark bronze colour. They are always sold in pairs. I use bacon to give the fish a lovely flavour. This recipe comes from the fishing village of Auchmithie near Arbroath.

Serves 4

1 pair of Arbroath smokies, backbone removed
freshly milled black pepper
Arran mustard
6 rashers of Ayrshire streaky bacon, rind removed (optional)
butter

Preheat the grill to a medium heat.

Season the smokies with black pepper and lightly coat with mustard. Cover them with the rashers of bacon, if using, and grill until the bacon is cooked or for three minutes on each side.

Unwrap the bacon, coat the fish with a little butter and serve with buttered toast.

orkney cheese and ayrshire bacon cake

This recipe gives you the opportunity to use the best of Scottish produce: Ayrshire bacon and Orkney cheese. A recipe similar to this was served to me at the Ballachulish Hotel, which is south of Fort William and north of Glencoe on the beautiful banks of Loch Linnhe. The area is unspoilt and the scenery breathtaking; the Ballachulish is one of those hotels I would visit for the Scottish breakfast alone.

Makes 8

150 g/6 oz rindless Ayrshire streaky bacon
225 g/8 oz self-raising flour
pinch salt
25 g/1 oz butter
100 g/4 oz Orkney cheese, grated
150 ml/⅓ pt milk
1 tbsp tomato ketchup
1 tsp Worcestershire sauce
1 tbsp milk, for glazing
watercress, for garnish
freshly milled black pepper

Preheat the oven to 200°C/400°F/Gas Mark 6.

Grill the bacon until crisp and cut into small pieces.

Sieve the flour and salt together, add the butter and rub together with your fingers until the mixture has the consistency of fine breadcrumbs. Add the bacon and one third of the cheese.

Mix the milk, ketchup and Worcestershire sauce and add to the dry ingredients to make a soft dough.

On a floured board, roll out an 18 cm/7 in. circle. Brush with milk and cut into 8 wedges.

Arrange on a greased baking tray and sprinkle with the remaining cheese. Bake in the centre of the oven for 20 minutes.

potato scones

This is the Scottish equivalent to the English potato cake or the Irish potato farl. I like to add a little grated cheddar to the mix and serve them with Ramsay's crispy grilled bacon and a fried egg.

Makes 8

450 g/1 lb mashed potato, hot and highly seasoned
50 g/2 oz butter
100 g/4 oz plain flour
50 g/2 oz Scottish Cheddar, grated (optional)
beef dripping, for frying

Place all the ingredients except the dripping in a bowl and blend thoroughly. Roll out the mixture on a floured board; cut into 10 cm/4 in. rounds and prick the surfaces with a fork.

Heat a little beef dripping in a large sauté pan and cook the scones for 3 to 4 minutes either side until golden brown.

Serve hot with lashings of butter.

old-fashioned bubble and squeak

Bubble and squeak was created in the seventeenth century and was originally a way of using up leftovers. The ingredients for the dish were placed in a dripping tray while the meat roasted on the front of the fire above. All the juices fell into the dripping tray, hence the name: bubble – from the juices dripping – and squeak – the noise of the roasting tin catching the juices.

Serves 4

450 g/1 lb mashed potato
225 g/8 oz cooked spring cabbage, chopped
225 g/8 oz chopped onion, cooked in a little butter
50 g/2 oz butter
salt
freshly ground white pepper

Combine the potato, cabbage and onion, and season. Heat the butter in a saucepan and fry the mixture for 5 minutes.

vegetable-filled bubble and squeak cakes

This recipe is a more sophisticated alternative to the simple, rustic version of bubble and squeak above. I came up with this idea after talking to several vegetarians who got bored with the very mundane dishes offered to them. The choice of filling is your own – the surprise centre makes this something special. I can recommend asparagus, or a mixture of sweetcorn, chopped tomatoes and spinach. A little grated cheese is a good addition, too.

Makes 8

25 ml/1 fl. oz cooking oil
1 medium onion, finely chopped
225 g/8 oz cooked cabbage, finely chopped
450 g/1 lb potatoes, cooked and mashed
freshly milled black pepper and salt

75 g/3 oz of your favourite vegetable, cooked
50 g/2 oz sifted plain flour
1 free-range egg beaten with a little milk
1 tbsp sesame or poppy seeds
1 tbsp vegetable oil

Heat the oil in a large frying pan and add the chopped onion. Cook for 3 minutes then add the cabbage and cook for a further 3 minutes. Finally, add the potatoes, season with salt and pepper, and fry over a medium heat for a further 10 minutes, blending the mixture during the cooking process.

Remove the mixture from the pan into a clean glass bowl and allow the mixture to cool.

Flour a cutting board and your hands. Take about 50 g/2 oz of the mixture, roll it into a ball and then flatten it like a pancake. Put a little of your chosen cooked vegetable onto the 'pancake' and fold it over, hiding the vegetable in the centre of the mixture.

Flatten and shape into a little round. Repeat this process with the rest of the mixture. Flour the cakes and brush them with the beaten egg, coat with some sesame seeds or poppy seeds then fry in the oil until golden brown, about 3 minutes either side.

aberdeen sausage

I found this recipe about 15 years ago in Ambrose Heath's *Good Breakfast Cookbook*, published by Faber & Faber in 1945.

Put a pound of lean beef and half a pound of fat bacon through the mincing machine twice, then mix well with a breakfast-cupful of breadcrumbs, a teaspoon of salt, and a quarter of a teaspoonful of pepper. Bind with a beaten egg and add if you like a dessertspoonful of Worcestershire sauce. Boil for two hours in a floured cloth (Clootie), and when the roll is done coat it in browned breadcrumbs as you would a piece of bacon.

scotch eggs

Although they used to be part of the Scots breakfast, today we tend to serve scotch eggs with a little mustard as an excellent quick lunch or supper snack. I use Argyll or Ayrshire pork sausage meat instead of ordinary sausage meat for a more robust savoury flavour. For something completely different, coat the eggs in the kipper paste on p. 52 and chill for 1 hour before serving.

Makes 6

6 medium-sized free-range eggs, hard-boiled and shelled	pinch marjoram
	pinch basil
50 g/2 oz seasoned flour	salt
350 g/12 oz Argyll pork sausage meat	freshly milled black pepper
1 tbsp chopped fresh parsley	1 free-range egg, beaten with a little milk
2 shallots, finely chopped	100 g/4 oz freshly toasted breadcrumbs
a little grated nutmeg	cooking oil (for deep frying)

Roll the eggs in the seasoned flour.

Place the sausage meat in a bowl with the parsley, shallots, nutmeg, marjoram, basil, salt and pepper, and work all the ingredients in together.

Divide the sausage meat into six equal portions; flatten the meat into six rounds, placing one egg onto each round. Work the meat around each egg with wet hands to form a smooth, even layer, ensuring that you seal the meat well.

Roll each egg in the seasoned flour, the egg wash and the breadcrumbs, and then repeat the process to ensure they are well coated.

Chill for 1 hour in the fridge and then heat the oil and deep fry for 6 minutes until they are golden brown, turning them every minute so that they cook evenly.

Remove the Scotch eggs with a slotted spoon onto some kitchen paper to remove the excess oil. Allow them to cool and serve with a rustic herb salad.

potted dunlop cheese with apple

A great summer recipe served with traditional beer and crusty bread or oatcakes.
Serves 4

1 apple
1 tbsp lemon juice
450 g/1 lb mellow Orkney cheese, grated
100 g/4 oz unsalted butter, softened
generous pinch powdered mace
1 tbsp Arran mustard
1 tbsp whisky

FOR THE CLARIFIED BUTTER:
225 g/8 oz unsalted butter

To prepare the clarified butter, heat the butter very slowly in a saucepan, skimming off the foam as the butter heats up. When the butter has completely melted, remove the pan from the heat and leave it to stand for 2 minutes, allowing the sediment to sink to the bottom.

Very slowly and carefully pour the clarified butter into a small container, leaving the sediment in the pan. The butter is then ready for use.

Dice the apple finely and mix in the lemon juice, which will prevent the apple from discolouring.

Mash all the ingredients for the potted cheese together thoroughly, or blend in a blender, until the mixture becomes very creamy in texture.

Add the apple and mix together.

Divide the mixture between earthenware dishes or ramekins, ensuring the cheese is pressed down firmly.

Top with clarified butter and leave in the refrigerator for at least two days.

kipper paste

Only good-quality kippers should be used for this recipe (the Loch Fyne seafood company is a good source of these – see Recommended Suppliers). Please do not use the yellow dyed fish or anything that comes in a plastic package from a supermarket shelf – fresh is good. You could also use naturally smoked salmon or finnan haddock. Take a look at my Scotch egg recipe (p. 50) for another interesting idea.

Serves 4

4–6 kippers, lightly grilled
100 g/4 oz butter, softened
juice of 1 lemon
freshly milled black pepper
salt
clarified butter (see potted Dunlop cheese, p. 51)

Remove the skin and bones from the grilled kippers and discard.

Put the butter and kippers into a bowl and blend thoroughly with a fork.

Add the lemon juice, black pepper and salt and blend again. Divide the mixture between ramekins and top with clarified butter.

Chill for 1 hour and then serve with crusty bread or warm toast and a bottle of Orkney Wine Company Black Portent. This wine is also good with cheese.

chicken and duck liver pâté

Use only good-quality livers from corn-fed chickens and wild ducks if possible when making your own pâté. I usually double the quantity of ingredients and make a big batch for friends and family.

Discard any discoloured pieces of liver, as they will be bitter. It is very important to taste and season the pâté before blending. Should you not like duck liver, double the quantity of chicken livers and vice versa. If you wish to store the pâté or freeze it, then top with clarified butter instead of lining with bacon.

Serves 4

340 g/12 oz butter
2 large red onions, very finely chopped
3 large garlic cloves, crushed
1 tsp sage
grated rind and juice of 1 orange
450 g/1 lb chicken livers, rinsed in cold water
450 g/1 lb duck livers, rinsed in cold water
salt
freshly milled black pepper
100 ml/3 fl. oz single malt whisky
225 g/8 oz naturally cured Argyll bacon, rind removed

Preheat the oven to 190°C/375°F/Gas Mark 5.

Melt the butter in a large, deep frying pan and gently fry the onion until it is transparent. Add the garlic, sage, orange juice and rind, and cook for 1 minute. Add the livers and cook for about 8 minutes. Add the salt and pepper with the whisky and cook for a further 4 minutes.

Mince the pâté in a blender or food processor.

Line an earthenware dish or non-stick loaf tin with the bacon, allowing the bacon to hang over the sides so that you can use it to cover the pâté. Add the pâté and cover with the bacon.

Place the dish in a large roasting tin with a little water and bake in the oven for 30 minutes.

Allow it to mature for at least a day before using. Serve with warm brown toast or with crackers.

loch lomond scots toast

Scots toast is a catch-all name for toasted bread with any one of a variety of toppings: finnan haddock, Arbroath smokies, cheese, minced game or pickled herrings. I devised this recipe while staying at our lodge on Loch Lomond and I declared it mouthwatering. It is quick and simple, and makes a very special breakfast. I use black-pudding bread but if you don't like black pudding, then use thick slices of white or brown bread instead.

Serves 2

8 rashers naturally cured Ayrshire bacon
4 slices black-pudding bread (see p. 192)
4 large free-range eggs
100 g/4 oz Dunlop cheese, grated
2 tbsp double cream
2 tbsp chopped spring onion
salt
freshly milled black pepper
100 g/4 oz Scottish butter

Preheat the oven to a low temperature and the grill to a medium heat.

Grill the bacon until crispy and toast the bread under the grill, then place them in the oven to keep warm.

Break the eggs into a bowl and beat them lightly, add the grated cheese, double cream and chopped spring onion, season well with salt and black pepper and mix thoroughly.

Melt half the butter in a large frying pan. Shake the pan so that the base is covered with hot frothing butter.

Pour the egg mixture into the pan, let it cook for 1 minute, then whisk with a fork until it is just cooked and still moist.

Spread the toast with the remaining butter and place a slice in the centre of each plate. Cut the other two pieces of toast into triangles and arrange them on the plates.

Divide the egg between the plates, top with crispy bacon and eat while piping hot.

scotch rarebit

I highly recommend serving the rarebit with a glass of Black Portent, a port-style blackcurrant wine made by the Orkney Wine Company. Fruit, cheese and port have always worked well together and this is a great combination.

Serves 4

225 g/8 oz Orkney cheese, grated
25 g/1 oz butter
1 tbsp Worcestershire sauce
1 tsp dried English mustard
1 tsp flour
4 tbsp stout
freshly milled black pepper
4 slices bread, toasted on one side only

Put the cheese, butter, Worcestershire sauce, mustard and flour into a saucepan, stirring well. Add the stout and black pepper, cook over a very gentle heat, stirring continuously, until smooth.

Place onto the untoasted side of the bread and brown under the grill.

A few rashers of naturally cured bacon, such as Ramsay of Carluke's, are a good accompaniment to this dish.

scotch woodcock

Another variation on the Scots toast theme, this recipe was introduced during the first half of the nineteenth century. It was simple to make and quite cheap, and became a Victorian classic, often served at the end of a meal.

Use high-quality tinned anchovies and free-range eggs for that traditional taste.
Serves 4

4 thick slices of bread
50 g/2 oz butter, softened
1 tbsp anchovy essence
2 x 75 g/3 oz tin anchovies, drained
4 free-range eggs
150 ml/⅓ pt double cream
salt
freshly milled black pepper
pinch cayenne pepper (optional)

Toast the bread and butter it well on both sides. Spread with the anchovy essence and then divide the drained anchovies between the four slices of toast, reserving 8 of them.

Beat the yolks of the eggs with the cream and season well with salt and pepper and the cayenne if liked. Pour the liquid slowly into a saucepan and heat gently, taking care only to thicken the egg rather than cooking it dry. Remove the saucepan from the heat and pour the creamed egg over the pieces of toast. Criss-cross with anchovies and serve immediately.

clapshot

Clapshot is a traditional dish of boiled mashed potatoes and turnips. In an article for *The Orcadian* entitled 'Stir up some pride in clapshot and respect our national dish', Alan Bichan writes:

> Clapshot could be regarded as Orkney's national dish. Although variations appear in other areas of the British Isles, it is in Orkney that it forms the greatest part of the staple diet.
>
> The origin of the word 'clapshot' remains a mystery. Some think the earliest form of the word was 'clatshop'. Others think it derived from the old Orkney word 'klepp' which was a small amount of a soft substance.
>
> Whatever its roots, there is no other foodstuff about which I am more passionate and, if I'm honest, more pernickety.

He goes on to recommend using a floury potato such as Yukon Gold or Premiere to offset the wetness of the turnip and to advise keeping the water in which the vegetables have been boiled to use in gravy or a pot of soup. He also suggests some delicious-sounding additions:

> A single parsnip will produce clapshot with character, while a carrot or two will add to the colour. The inclusion of fried leeks at the mashing stage is also worth a try and nutmeg works well as an extra seasoning.

Here is my recipe for a basic clapshot.
Serves 4

700 g/1½ lb potatoes, diced
700 g/1½ lb turnips, diced
50 g/2 oz butter
1 tbsp double cream
salt
freshly milled black pepper
2 tbsp freshly snipped chives

Cook the potatoes and turnips in boiling salted water until tender and drain them well.
Mash them with the butter and cream, season well with salt and pepper, and sprinkle with chives.

highland beef sausages and mash

This is a very versatile recipe that you see in every type of restaurant. I tried this version in The Living Room in Edinburgh, which is owned by a dear friend of mine, Tim Bacon.

Use your favourite beef sausages for this recipe. Mine are Aberdeen Angus from the Isle of Islay – the fame of our British banger will never die!

Serve this with Orkney Elderberry Borealis. The elderberry flavours are wonderful with the beef sausage – in fact, this wine is good with any rich beef dish.

Serves 4

25 g/1 oz beef dripping
12 thick beef sausages
900 g/2 lb potatoes, peeled and boiled
50 g/2 oz butter
1 onion, chopped
1 tbsp chopped fresh parsley
freshly grated nutmeg
salt

Preheat the oven to 150°C/300°F/Gas Mark 2.

Heat the oil or dripping in a large frying pan. Prick the sausages with a fork in three different places and gently fry them, cooking them until golden brown all over, about 6 minutes. Place the sausages in a deep serving dish and put them in the oven at a low temperature to keep warm.

Meanwhile, reheat the boiled potatoes in boiling water. Melt the butter in a large saucepan and gently fry the onion for 3 minutes. Drain the boiled potatoes and mash them with the onions and butter. Add the parsley, a little freshly grated nutmeg and salt to taste, blend into the potatoes and place in another serving dish. Serve with onion gravy, for which a recipe is given on p. 23.

aberdeen angus meatballs
in onion gravy

Also known as Highland beef balls, in the early eighteenth century these were cooked in ox skins and eaten as a breakfast or supper dish. The recipe was originally invented to use up leftover trimmings from the rump, sirloin and rib-eye.

Today, meatballs can be purchased in any food store but they do not have the flavour of home-made ones. Use your favourite meat, minced – lamb, pork or chicken – should you not want to use beef.

Serves 4

1 large red onion, chopped
450 g/1 lb minced Aberdeen Angus rump steak
1 tsp paprika
50 g/2 oz beef suet
75 g/3 oz stale white breadcrumbs
pinch ground ginger
pinch ground cloves
salt
freshly milled black pepper
2 tbsp olive oil
50 g/2 oz butter
onion gravy (see p. 23)

Preheat the oven to 180°C/350°F/Gas Mark 4.

Make the onion gravy in advance.

Combine the onion, beef, paprika, suet and breadcrumbs, and blend thoroughly. Season with the ginger, cloves, salt and pepper. Flour your hands and shape the mixture into 14 large meatballs.

Heat the olive oil and butter in a large frying pan, add the meatballs and cook until they are completely brown all over.

Place the meatballs in a deep casserole dish, pour over the onion gravy, cover and bake in the centre of the oven for 25 minutes.

black pudding

Puddins a' hot, a' hot,
Pipin' hot, pipin' hot!
Hot or cold, they must be sold,
Puddins a' hot, a' hot!

Old Edinburgh Street Cry

I was quite surprised to discover that the Scots, just like the people of Lancashire, enjoy black pudding. I have Scottish recipes dating back to 1715, when a sausage made from bullock's blood and barley meal with pepper and ginger was described as blood pudding. In the west of Scotland, they use bullock's or sheep's blood with mint, wrapped in tripe skins.

Ramsay of Carluke have been making the original pig's-blood recipe for years and it is more popular now than ever. Fried in butter and served with potato scones and rashers of naturally cured bacon, it is an essential part of the Scottish breakfast.

I am not for one minute suggesting you try the old methods of making black pudding but they are amusing to read.

Before you kill a hog, get a peck of groats [oats], boil them half an hour in water, then drain them, and put them in a clean tub or large pan.

Then kill your hog, save two quarts of the cold blood, and keep stirring it till it is quite cold: then mix it with your groats, and stir them well together. Season with a large teaspoon of salt, a quarter ounce of cloves, mace and nutmeg together, an equal quantity of each; dry it, beat it well and mix in.

The next day take the leaf (fat) of the hog, and cut it into dice, scrape, and wash the guts very clean, then tie one end. And begin to fill them, but be sure to put in a good deal of fat, fill the skins three parts full, tie the other end, and make your puddings what length you please; prick them with a pin, and put them in a kettle of boiling water. Boil them slowly for an hour, then take them out and lay them on straw.

The Frugal Housewife, 1811

black pudding and potato with mustard sauce

Sauce is the soul of food and I am sure you will appreciate this very novel recipe, which was given to me by Jacqueline Ramsay at Ramsay of Carluke.

Serves 4

4 good-quality Scottish black puddings
4 large potatoes, peeled, boiled and thickly sliced
2 onions, thinly sliced
50 g/2 oz butter
2 apples, peeled, cored and sliced
50 g/2 oz plain flour
100 ml/3 fl. oz coarse-grain mustard
1 tbsp English mustard
300 ml/½ pt beef stock (see p. 14)
pinch nutmeg
pinch thyme
salt
freshly milled black pepper
100 g/4 oz cheddar cheese, grated

Preheat the oven to 200°C/400°F/Gas Mark 6.

Slice the black pudding 2–3 cm/1 in. in thickness. Remove any skin from the slices of pudding.

Line a deep baking dish with the slices of potato.

In a saucepan, fry the onions in the butter. Remove them with a slotted spoon, retaining the butter in the pan for later, and place them over the potato, covering it completely.

Add the slices of apple to the dish on top of the onions, then finish off with the black pudding.

Put the flour and mustards into the pan in which the onions were fried and cook for 2 minutes. Slowly add the stock, stirring constantly until the sauce is smooth. Sprinkle with nutmeg and thyme, taste, and season with salt and pepper.

Finally, pour the sauce over the black pudding, sprinkle with the grated cheese and bake in the oven for 20 minutes.

fat-free black pudding with bramley apple

I make this recipe at least once a month. I get the dried blood from a black-pudding maker in Lancashire. You will also need black-pudding sleeves, which any good butcher should be able to supply. Should you not wish to go to the trouble of making it yourself, have a look at the Recommended Suppliers list at the back of the book. Many butchers sell black pudding by mail order or via their websites.

Serves 4

115 g/4 oz oatmeal
50 g/2 oz barley flour
50 g/2 oz cooked pearl barley
1 small onion, finely chopped
700 g/1 lb 9 oz dried pig's blood
115 g/4 oz castor sugar
1 litre/1¾ pt hot water
1 tbsp lemon juice
1 large/2 small Bramley apples, cut into small
dice
salt
freshly milled black pepper
generous pinch mace
generous pinch nutmeg
1 tsp fresh thyme, finely chopped

Place the oatmeal, barley flour, cooked pearl barley, onion and pig's blood into a large pan or bowl and slowly blend in the hot water; add the lemon juice and Bramley apple and stir thoroughly for 5 minutes. Add the seasoning, herbs and spices, blending thoroughly, and allow the mixture to cool.

Place the black-pudding mixture into the black-pudding sleeves, ensuring they are tightly packed and tied securely. Poach them slowly in a large saucepan of simmering water for 35 minutes.

Remove the black puddings and allow them to cool naturally. If you are not using them straight away, put them in an airtight container in the fridge and use when required. They will keep for 4 days.

Otherwise, slice and lightly grill, serve with bubble and squeak (see p. 48), and my mustard and whisky sauce (see p. 25).

game

The quality of game in Scotland is without doubt second to none and I truly enjoy creating recipes with venison, hare and rabbit. The term game was traditionally applied only to wild birds and animals that were hunted for food, such as partridge, pheasant, hare, rabbit and venison. Farmed game is now widely available from butchers and supermarkets, and includes venison, guinea fowl and quail. Wild game is subject to legal shooting seasons (see table on next page) but farmed game is available all year round. You can buy wild game from specialist suppliers, wholesale markets, or direct from a shoot or estate which has a selling licence.

To me, venison is the meat of kings. I have cooked it every way possible but still like the idea of slow-cooked or braised haunch of venison, known in Scotland as 'Rob Roy's Pleesure'. This succulent piece of venison would have been pot-roasted in a three-legged iron pot with vegetables and herbs grown naturally in the Highlands – a dish enjoyed by generations of hunters and raiders like Rob Roy MacGregor.

Nichola Fletcher, who owns Fletchers of Auchtermuchty, knows all about venison and game; Nichola wrote the bestselling book *Game For All* in 1987. As artisan food producers, the Fletchers have been refining the quality of their venison for 30 years. A couple of years ago they were nominated for a Slow Food Award in recognition of this. Nichola told me: 'Do bear in mind we are just a wee family business, not a huge multinational – which is why our venison is so good.'

Writing in his *Cook's Oracle* in 1817, William Kitchiner got to the heart of what makes game meat so special:

> Game and other wild animals proper for food are of very superior qualities to the tame, from the total contrast of the circumstances attending them. They have a free range of exercise in the open air, and choose their own food, the good effects of which are very evident in a short delicate texture of flesh, found only in them.
>
> Their juices and flavour are more pure, and their fat, when it is in any degree, as in venison, and some other instances, differs as much from that of our fatted animals as silver and gold from the grosser metals. The superiority of Welsh mutton and Scotch beef is owing to a similar cause.

GAME SEASONS	
blackcock	October–December
duck	all year
duck, wild	August–January
duckling	March–September
goose	September–March
gosling	March–September
grouse	August–December
guinea fowl	October–February
hare	August–February
partridge	September–February
pheasant	October–February
pigeon	August–April
ptarmigan	December–May
quail	June–August
rabbit	all year
salmon	February–October
trout	February–September
turkey	all year
venison	May–October
wild boar	all year
woodcock	August–March

traditional roast venison

The best cuts for roasting are the haunch and saddle. Allow 25 minutes per lb for roasting.

If you have cold roast venison left over, the following, from Hannah Wolley's *The Accomplish't Lady's Delight* (1675), is a great way to use it up:

> Put it in a stewing dish and set it on a heap of coals with a little claret wine, a sprig or two of Rosemary, half a dozen cloves, a little grated bread, Sugar and Vinegar, so let it stew together awhile, then grate on Nutmeg and dish it up.

Serves 6

2.3 kg/5 lb haunch Scottish venison
175 g/6 oz butter
rind and juice of 1 orange
8 cloves
25 g/1 oz seasoned flour
6 sprigs fresh rosemary, to decorate

FOR THE MARINADE:
300 ml/½pt red wine
1 carrot, peeled and sliced
1 large red onion, peeled and sliced

1 leek, sliced
2 sprigs of fresh thyme
1 bay leaf
6 juniper berries
1 tsp freshly grated ginger
1 tsp black peppercorns
3 tbsp balsamic vinegar
3 tbsp olive oil
2 cloves garlic
2 tbsp warm heather honey

Place all the marinade ingredients in a large saucepan, bring to the boil and simmer for 15 minutes. Allow the marinade to cool.

Place the haunch into a large, deep serving dish, pour over the marinade, cover and leave in a cool place for 24 hours, turning the venison every 6 hours.

Set the oven to 180°C/350°F/Gas Mark 4.

Remove the venison from the marinade and set the marinade aside to use later in the sauce. Spread the venison with the butter, scatter over the orange rind, pour over the orange juice and stick in the cloves. Place in a deep roasting tray and cook for 2 hours, basting every 30 minutes.

Remove the venison from the roasting tin, place on a large serving dish and keep warm in the oven until the sauce is made.

Pour the juices from the venison into a saucepan, add the flour and cook for 2 minutes. Slowly add the marinade, bring to the boil and reduce by half.

Strain the sauce through a fine sieve into a sauceboat and serve with the venison. Garnish the joint with sprigs of fresh rosemary and put out a jar of rowan jelly. If you'd like to make your own, there is a recipe on p. 223.

venison casserole
with blaeberry hairst

This type of casserole is always better when left for at least 24 hours. For extra flavour, marinate the venison in the game stock and Blaeberry Hairst, which is a full-bodied, smooth blueberry wine, for at least 12 hours before cooking.

Blaeberry Hairst is available from the Orkney Wine Company (see Recommended Suppliers).

Serves 4

    100 g/4 oz rindless streaky bacon
    50 g/2 oz butter
    900 g/2 lb venison, diced
    4 potatoes, peeled and chopped
    450 g/1 lb shallots, peeled
    2 carrots, sliced
    100 g/4 oz wild mushrooms, roughly chopped
    1 tsp thyme
    1 tsp wild rosemary
    salt
    freshly milled black pepper
    pinch cayenne pepper
    600 ml/1 pt game stock (see p. 16)
    150 ml/⅓ pt Blaeberry Hairst
    1 tbsp softened butter
    1 tbsp plain flour

Preheat the oven to 160°C/325°F/Gas Mark 3.

Trim the bacon, cutting each rasher into 5 or 6 pieces. Place the bacon with the butter in a casserole and place in the oven. After 3 minutes, add the venison and cook for 5 minutes.

Now add the vegetables, sprinkle with the herbs and season well with salt, pepper and a generous pinch of cayenne. Cook for a further 10 minutes.

Pour over the stock and Blaeberry Hairst, and simmer for 90 minutes.

In a small saucepan, melt the butter, sprinkle over the flour, stir and cook for 5 minutes to make a roux.

Stir the roux into the casserole to thicken the juices, simmering for a further 10 minutes.

Allow the casserole to stand for 10 minutes before serving.

grilled steaks of perthshire venison tam's brig

I created this recipe on my first visit to Kinloch Rannoch in Perth in the 1960s. I have used it at numerous garden parties around the world ever since.

I would use a good grainy mustard here such as an Arran mustard, or Macallan whisky mustard, which can be found in good delicatessens.

Serves 4

4 x 255 g/9 oz Perthshire venison steaks

FOR THE MARINADE:
150 ml/5 fl. oz claret
2 cloves garlic, crushed
2 tbsp clear heather honey
2 tbsp mustard
2 shallots, peeled and chopped
1 tsp mild curry powder
1 tsp celery salt
4 tbsp sesame oil
1 tbsp crushed almonds
freshly milled black pepper

In a glass bowl, blend all the marinade ingredients together thoroughly.

Tenderise the steaks with a meat tenderiser or rolling pin. Coat each steak with the marinade and place them in a deep plate. Cover completely with the remaining marinade and leave in a cool place for 24 hours, turning the steaks occasionally.

Grill or barbecue for 4 to 5 minutes each side (to your taste), basting with the marinade. Serve with redcurrant jelly, sliced mushrooms fried in a little butter, and lots of good claret.

braised venison
with horseradish dumplings

Braised venison really is a great winter dish and the horseradish in the dumplings gives a lovely warm, spicy flavour. I recommend serving this with clapshot – mashed potatoes and turnips (see p. 57).

Serves 4

4 x 285 g/10 oz venison cutlets or steaks
450 g/1 lb onions, peeled and diced
2 large carrots, peeled and diced
100 g/4 oz swede, peeled and diced
150 ml/⅓ pt brown ale
1 tsp tomato purée
600 ml/1 pt beef or game stock (see pp. 14 and 16)
salt
freshly milled black pepper
sprig of rosemary

FOR THE DUMPLINGS:
225 g/8 oz plain flour
100 g/4 oz vegetable suet
salt
25 g/1 oz freshly grated horseradish
6 tbsp water

Preheat the oven to 200°C/400°F/Gas Mark 6.

Put the venison in a deep ovenproof casserole dish and scatter over the vegetables.

Pour the brown ale, tomato purée and meat stock into a bowl, season with salt and pepper, and blend thoroughly. Pour the liquid over the meat and vegetables, and add the sprig of rosemary. Cover with cooking foil, place in the centre of the oven and braise for 90 minutes.

Meanwhile, make up the dumplings: sift the flour into a clean bowl, add the suet and horseradish, season well with salt, mix together and then sprinkle in the water. Stir with a fork to form a soft dough.

Turn out the mixture onto a floured board and shape it into small balls about the size of walnuts. Set aside until the 90 minutes' cooking time is up.

Remove the cooking foil and give the venison a good stir, turning each cutlet. Add the dumplings and return to the oven for a further 30 minutes.

Serve with clapshot (see p. 57).

confit of duck in goose or duck fat

You can purchase goose fat from most supermarkets today and I do know that Jenners at Loch Lomond Shores sells it (see Recommended Suppliers). If you have duck fat then do use that; it is also excellent for roasting potatoes.

Serves 4

10 duck legs (from wild ducks if you can get them)
75 g/3 oz rock salt
500 g/1 lb goose or duck fat
2 tbsp honey
1 tsp sesame seeds

FOR THE MARINADE:
4 tbsp soy sauce
2 tbsp balsamic vinegar
5 cloves garlic, peeled and sliced
5 cm/3 in. piece root ginger, peeled and sliced
1 sprig thyme
1 sprig rosemary

Sprinkle the duck legs with rock salt and put in a dish. Cover the dish and refrigerate overnight.

Rinse the duck legs and dry with absorbent kitchen paper. Place in a dish with the marinade ingredients. Cover the dish and marinate the duck legs for 24 hours or overnight in the refrigerator.

Preheat the oven to 160°C/325°F/Gas Mark 3.

Remove the duck legs from the marinade and dry them with paper towel. Put them in a large ovenproof dish and pour over the goose or duck fat. Place the dish in the oven for 2 hours until the meat falls easily away from the bone.

Remove the legs from the fat. Pass the fat through a muslin-lined sieve into a clean bowl. When cool, pour into sealed containers and refrigerate for future use.

Turn the oven up to 220°C/425°F/Gas Mark 8.

Place the duck legs on a baking tray, trickle over the honey and sprinkle with sesame seeds, then place in the oven for 10 minutes.

breast of wild duckling with a sage and rowanberry honey sauce

One of my favourite places to visit when I am in Edinburgh is The Living Room restaurant and cocktail bar. The owner, Tim Bacon, is a very special person with a vast knowledge of the restaurant business, and food and drink in general.

Here is a recipe from The Living Room with all the flavours of Edinburgh Farmers' Market. It is a fact that Scots honey is the best in the world, not because Scottish bees know how to make it any better than other bees, but because of the quality and excellence of the clover and heather, which is particularly full in nectar.

Serves 4

4 x 275 g/10 oz (preferably wild) duckling breast fillets, trimmed
salt
freshly milled black pepper
25 g/1 oz butter
½ tsp dried sage
1 tbsp chopped fresh sage
1 small carrot, finely chopped
75 g/3 oz shallots, thinly sliced
1 tbsp lemon juice
4 tbsp heather honey
100 g/4 oz fresh or frozen rowanberries
25 g/1 oz flour
1 tbsp Worcestershire sauce
150 ml/⅓ pt chicken stock

Score the fat of the duck breasts with a sharp knife and season them well all over.

Heat the butter in a frying pan and seal the meat, cooking for 3 minutes on either side.

Add the sage, carrot, shallots and lemon juice.

Add half of the chicken stock, let it simmer for 1 minute then add half of the honey and half of the rowanberries and a sprinkling of flour. Allow to cook for 3 minutes, season with freshly ground black pepper and add the Worcestershire sauce.

Now add the rest of the chicken stock and cook for a minute before adding the remaining honey and berries, allowing 3 minutes' cooking time.

Remove the meat from the pan, allowing the sauce to continue simmering for 4 minutes.

Slice the duck breast lengthways into ½ cm/¼ in. pieces.

Pour a little of the sauce onto each serving plate, arrange the breast slices in a fan shape and decorate with fresh sage leaves and some fresh berries.

COOKING HARE OR RABBIT

There are two types of hare: the English, which is often called the brown hare; and the blue hare, which is Scottish. Older hares are ideal for casseroles, as their meat benefits from being marinated before cooking. Younger hares are very good for a roast and simply need basting with a little butter. The hare's teeth are the clue to its age: the leveret, or young hare, will have small white teeth and the oldie will have large yellow ones. Hares, old or young, should be hung head downwards, ungutted, for one week.

Rabbits, the really wild ones, have a gamey flavour. Older ones can be hung for up to one week. The young rabbit, however, should be skinned and used within two days and must not be hung. Rabbit, both farmed and wild, is widely available throughout the year. It is a highly versatile meat and may be simply roasted, casseroled, curried, fried or made into pies and pâtés. It is very low in fat and a particularly healthy meat to eat.

Your butcher will skin a hare or rabbit for you or you can do it yourself: gut the hare or rabbit and remove the innards. Sever all four legs at the first joint. Cut through the skin around the hind legs, just below the tail, peeling the skin down off the hind legs. Tie the hind legs together and place on a firm hook; pull the skin down over the body to the end of the forelegs. Remove the head and wash the body with cold water. Rub salt into the cavity and over the complete carcass, and leave for one hour. Wash thoroughly again and then cut the hare or rabbit into joints.

roasted rabbit

Young rabbit is preferable for roasting.
   Serves 4

   1 rabbit approx. 450 g/1 lb in weight

   FOR THE MARINADE:
   450 ml/¾ pt red wine
   1 large onion, sliced
   3 cloves garlic
   2 tbsp lemon juice
   60 ml/2 fl. oz olive oil
   sprig of rosemary
   6 juniper berries
   salt
   freshly milled black pepper

Mix all the marinade ingredients together in a deep bowl, completely cover the rabbit and chill for 12 hours.
   Preheat the oven to 200°C/400°F/Gas Mark 6.
   Put the rabbit with the marinade in a roasting tin and cook for around 40 to 60 minutes, basting the meat with the marinade every 15 minutes. Cut the meat into 4 portions and serve.

jugged hare
with potato herb dumplings

This recipe replicates one of the oldest methods in Scottish cookery: game or other meat was placed in a jug with a marinade, then the jug was covered and sat in a pot half-filled with water, which was boiled for several hours.

According to my mother, my grandmother made this on a regular basis in the 1930s and served it with chunky farmhouse bread.

Serves 4

50 g/2 oz butter
75 g/3 oz rindless streaky bacon, chopped
675 g/1½ lb hare meat or 1 large hare,
    jointed
1 onion, roughly chopped
2 carrots, peeled and diced
2 sticks celery, chopped
zest of half a lemon
salt
freshly milled black pepper
600 ml/1 pt chicken stock (see p. 15)
25 g/1 oz plain flour
150 ml/¼ pt port

FOR THE DUMPLINGS:
350 g/12 oz mashed potato, seasoned
1 free-range egg, beaten
salt
freshly milled black pepper
generous pinch mixed herbs
50 g/2 oz seasoned flour
25 g/1 oz semolina
2 tbsp milk

In a bowl, mix all the ingredients for the dumplings thoroughly, seasoning well. Shape into small balls about the size of walnuts and place to one side until required.

Add the butter and bacon to a large saucepan and cook for 3 minutes. Add the hare and cook for 7 minutes, until the hare is browned, then add the vegetables and lemon zest, and season well with salt and pepper.

Pour over the stock and half the port, bring to the boil and then reduce the heat. Place a lid which is slightly smaller than the pan on top of the meat and weigh it down with something heavy. Simmer for 3 hours on a low heat.

Mix the flour with a little port to make a paste and add to the pan, cook for 3 minutes and add the rest of the port. Add the dumplings, cover and simmer for a further 20 minutes.

Serve with crusty bread and a bottle of dry red wine.

hare in a mushroom and red wine sauce

I have seen this recipe completely ruined by overcooking or because cheap wine has been used. One should always use a good quality burgundy for hare and rabbit recipes to express the true character of the dish.

This dish was popular with the gentry in the nineteenth century; my version has been adapted to take into account the modern trend towards healthy eating.

Serves 4

2.3 kg/5 lb hare, skin removed, jointed into 8 pieces
2 tbsp olive oil
100 g/4 oz streaky bacon, cut into pieces
225 g/8 oz shallots, peeled
225 g/8 oz button mushrooms, trimmed
3 tbsp seasoned flour
2 garlic cloves, finely chopped
sprig of thyme
4 tbsp finely chopped parsley, plus a little extra to garnish
1 bay leaf
salt
freshly milled black pepper
4 tbsp brandy
1 bottle good burgundy wine

Preheat the oven to 160°C/325°F/Gas Mark 3.

Cut the hare into bitesize pieces, making sure that all the excess fat and skin is removed. In a large ovenproof casserole, heat the olive oil and sauté the pieces of bacon. After two minutes, add the shallots and mushrooms.

Cook for a further 3 minutes then remove the bacon, shallots and mushrooms from the casserole onto a warm plate.

Toss the pieces of hare in the seasoned flour and sauté for 10 minutes, turning every 3 minutes.

Add the game stock, bacon, shallots, mushrooms, garlic, thyme, parsley and bay leaf, and season the casserole with salt and pepper. Cover the casserole and place in the oven for 60 minutes.

Remove the hare pieces, bacon and vegetables from the casserole and keep them warm. Skim off any excess fat from the hare juices, pour in the warmed brandy and ignite, allowing it to burn out for at least two minutes.

Pour over the burgundy wine, saving at least one glassful. Cook the wine until it is reduced by half the original quantity. Add a little of the reserved wine to the cornflour, making it into a paste; add the cornflour to the sauce, whisking it in.

Let the sauce cook for 4 minutes, then strain it into a clean casserole, adding the hare, bacon and vegetables. Let it simmer in the oven for a further 35 minutes. Garnish with chopped parsley and serve with garlic croutons and game chips. Game chips are deep-fried thinly sliced potatoes – good-quality crisps, essentially – and can be bought ready-made in supermarkets and delicatessens.

rabbit cooked in port with a creamy whisky and orange sauce

A friend of mine, Peter Smith, who owns the Cross Gaits Inn, one of the oldest pubs in the north of England, loves using whisky in his sauces. When I first saw this recipe on his menu, I thought, 'This is not going to work.' Peter told me he found it on a visit to Ballinluig, near where Rob Roy escaped from jail in 1717. After tasting the sauce with the rabbit, I could see why this is so popular not only at the Ballinluig Inn in Perthshire but also at the Cross Gaits near Blacko, Lancashire. Scottish food does travel well!

I suggest using Famous Grouse whisky for this recipe as it is a good robust whisky, not too expensive, which will stand up to the other flavours in the dish.

Serves 4

meat of 2 small rabbits (approx. 700 g/1 ½ lb)
50 g/2 oz butter
150 g/5 oz rindless cured bacon, chopped
2 tbsp port
150 ml/⅓ pt game stock (see p. 16)
zest and juice of 2 large oranges
salt
freshly milled black pepper
2 tbsp whisky
150 ml/⅓ pt sour cream

Cut the rabbit meat into thin slices, each weighing 25 g/1 oz, giving approximately 6 per serving.

Heat the butter in a frying pan, add the rabbit and cook gently for 10 minutes, turning frequently, until the meat is lightly coloured. Add the bacon and port, and cook for a further 8 minutes.

Remove the rabbit and bacon from the pan, arrange in a spiral shape on a large serving plate and keep warm.

Return the pan with the juices from the rabbit to the heat. Add the game stock, orange juice and zest, and reduce by half. Season with salt and pepper, add the whisky and cook for a further 5 minutes. Finally, add the cream and reduce by half.

Pour the sauce into the centre of the rabbit spiral and serve immediately with some fresh asparagus and new potatoes.

breast of maize-fed squab pigeon with a whisky sauce

A neighbour of mine, Jim Jackson, flies pigeons to and from the Continent with Orrell and District Homing Society. He tells me that squab (young pigeon) for eating should be 10 to 14 days old. All Jim's pigeons are fed on New Zealand maple peas and Cribbs maize.

I first tasted whole roast squab pigeon at Inverlochy Castle in Torlundy, near Fort William. It is a grand place with views of Ben Nevis and well worth a visit. This particular recipe is very popular at the Balmoral Hotel in Edinburgh.

Should you not be able to get squab, then use normal pigeon breast and add an extra 5 minutes' cooking time.

Serves 4

25 g/1 oz butter
12 squab pigeon breasts
1 small carrot, finely chopped
50 g/2 oz shallots, finely chopped
1 tbsp lemon juice
150 ml/¼ pt chicken stock (see p. 15)

90 ml/3 fl. oz single malt whisky
100 g/4 oz fresh or tinned black cherries
25 g/1 oz flour
salt
freshly milled black pepper
1 tbsp Worcestershire sauce

Heat the butter in a frying pan and seal the pigeon breasts, cooking for about 4 minutes.

Add the carrot, shallots, lemon juice and a little of the stock. Let it simmer for 4 minutes then add the rest of the stock, the whisky and the cherries and sprinkle over the flour. Allow to cook for 4 minutes, season with salt and pepper, and add the Worcestershire sauce.

Remove the meat from the pan, allowing the sauce to continue simmering for 5 minutes.

Pour a little of the sauce onto a serving plate, arrange the breast meat in a fan shape and decorate with fresh cherries and a slice of apple. Serve the rest of the sauce separately so that people can help themselves.

pheasant with rosemary and cider sauce

This recipe should be served with game chips, or a creamy mashed potato with some apple purée mixed through it to help soak up those mouthwatering juices.

Serves 4

8 slices of rindless streaky bacon
8 pheasant breasts
8 wooden cocktail sticks
1 tbsp chopped wild rosemary
1 large onion, sliced
300 ml/½ pt dry cider
150 ml/¼ pt espagnole sauce (see p. 21)
2 tbsp heather honey, warmed

1 tbsp English mustard
1 tsp tomato purée
salt
freshly milled black pepper
1 tbsp butter

FOR THE GARNISH:
1 apple, sliced
1 sprig fresh rosemary

Preheat the oven to 240°C/450°F/Gas Mark 9.

Wrap a slice of bacon around each piece of pheasant and secure with a wooden cocktail stick. Place the pieces in a deep, buttered casserole and cook uncovered in the oven for 15 minutes. Remove the cocktail sticks.

In a bowl, thoroughly mix the rosemary, onion, cider, espagnole sauce, honey, mustard, tomato purée, salt and pepper. Pour the mixture over the pheasant and cover with a lid. Lower the oven temperature to 150°C/300°F/Gas Mark 2 and put the casserole in the centre of the oven for 60 minutes.

In a small saucepan, melt the butter, sprinkle over the flour, stir and cook for 5 minutes to make a roux.

Meanwhile, remove the pheasant and bacon to a warm serving dish, pour the sauce into a saucepan and heat.

Mix the roux into the sauce and cook, stirring, for a few minutes, until the sauce has thickened slightly.

Pour the hot sauce around the pheasant and garnish with slices of apple and the rosemary.

ghillie's hotpot

This classic dish was created to use up any leftover game; ghillie is the term for a Highland gamekeeper. I first tasted this at a venison shoot in the early 1980s. You can use any game meat for this recipe: the Lairhillock Inn, near Aberdeen, make their hotpot with wild boar and venison.

Serves 4

50 g/2 oz beef dripping
900 g/2 lb mixed game meat, in large chunks
salt
freshly milled black pepper
2 or 3 large red onions, sliced
I small swede, diced
I large carrot, diced
25 g/I oz plain flour
600 ml/I pt beef stock (see p. 14)
II5 ml/4 fl. oz port
I sprig rosemary
2 cloves
900 g/2 lb potatoes, peeled and thinly sliced

Preheat the oven to 190°C/375°F/Gas Mark 5.

Heat the dripping in a large frying pan and quickly brown the game meat, cooking for about 5 minutes. Remove the game meat to a large ovenproof casserole, season well and keep warm in a low oven.

Crush the rosemary and cloves using a pestle and mortar.

In the same frying pan, cook the onions until they become transparent, about 3 minutes, add the swede, carrot and flour and cook for 2 minutes. Slowly add the beef stock and port, season well with salt and pepper, and add the rosemary and cloves, stirring all the time.

Remove the meat from the oven and layer it in the casserole with the potatoes.

Pour over the stock mixture, cover with a tight-fitting lid and cook in the centre of the oven for 2 hours.

Take off the lid for the last 15 minutes to brown the potatoes.

pan-fried breast of red-legged partridge with skirlie and red wine giblet sauce

While Hannah Wolley wrote in *The Accomplish't Lady's Delight* (1675), that 'the flavour of partridge is like that of no other game bird and must be treated with respect', Mrs Marshall thought in her *Cookery Book* of 1888 that 'Partridge, Grouse, Ptarmigan and Blackcock, must be treated and served in the same manner as pheasants'. Whatever your view, partridge is certainly delicious. The best version of this recipe I ever tasted was at the Road Hole Grill at the Old Course Hotel in the historic town of St Andrews, Fife.

Skirlie is a traditional dish of oatmeal stir-fried in a pan, often used as a stuffing.

Serves 4

8 red-legged partridges, or 8 x 75 g/3 oz partridge breasts
1 tbsp olive oil

FOR THE SKIRLIE:
50 g/2 oz dripping
1 medium red onion, finely chopped
125 g/4½ oz medium or coarse oatmeal

FOR THE SAUCE:
300 ml/½ pt red wine
2 tbsp redcurrant jelly
600 ml/1 pt giblet stock (see p. 17)
salt
freshly milled black pepper
25 g/1 oz butter, chilled and diced

Partridge breasts are easy to remove. First, cut off the legs through the joint next to the ribcage. Then, with a small sharp knife, cut along the breastbone and with small swift strokes, keeping parallel to the breastbone, gradually ease the flesh away and release it from the carcass. Pull off the skin and they are ready to cook. Reserve one of the carcasses, as it will be used to flavour the sauce.

To make the sauce, put the red wine and jelly in a large saucepan and reduce to about 2 tablespoons. Add the giblet stock, place the carcass of one of the partridges in the pan and gently simmer, reducing the stock by half. Strain, removing the carcass and any small bones, into a clean saucepan. Taste and season. Blend in the butter and simmer for 2 minutes. Keep warm but do not allow the sauce to boil

For the skirlie, melt the fat in a frying pan and add the onion. Cook over a gentle heat until just beginning to turn golden. Stir in the oatmeal and 'skirl' it around the pan (in other words, keep it moving) for a couple of minutes until the fat is absorbed and the oatmeal is cooked. Keep warm.

Season the breasts well with salt and pepper. Warm a heavy-based frying pan until very hot. Add 1 tablespoon of oil to the pan, then the breasts, skinned side down. Fry for 4 minutes then turn over and fry for 4 minutes more. Take the pan off the heat onto a cold surface, allowing the partridge to rest for a few minutes.

Carefully slice the partridge breasts with a sharp knife. Set the slices on top of the skirlie and pour around the red wine giblet sauce.

breast of guinea fowl
with chive sauce

The guinea fowl is like a cross between a corn-fed chicken and a pheasant, a very versatile and appetising bird which is delicious roasted or barbecued. I must say it is one of my favourite things to have when I visit restaurants in Scotland.

Serves 4

50 g/2 oz butter

4 x 225 g/8 oz guinea fowl fillets, trimmed

1 tbsp lemon juice

150 ml/⅓ pt chicken stock (see p. 15)

50 ml/2 fl. oz white wine

salt

freshly milled black pepper

25 g/1 oz flour

6 tbsp cream

1 tbsp chopped chives, plus a little extra to garnish

Preheat the oven to 190°C/375°F/Gas Mark 5.

Heat the butter in the frying pan and brown the breasts of guinea fowl. Add the lemon juice and a little of the stock. Let it simmer for 4 minutes then add the wine and seasoning. Allow to cook for a further 5 minutes and then place the breasts on a warm serving dish in the preheated oven until required.

Allow the sauce to continue simmering. Add the flour, the rest of the chicken stock, the cream and the chives, and cook for 10 minutes. Allow the sauce to rest for 5 minutes.

Pour a little of the sauce onto individual hot plates, remove the guinea fowl from the oven and place on the plates. Add a little more chive sauce and serve with baby carrots and broccoli. Sprinkle with chives.

roast grouse with bacon and dripping triangles

Grouse is the first game bird to come into season, on 12 August – the 'Glorious Twelfth'. This is two weeks before partridge and six weeks before pheasant. It is a native of wild heather moorlands, giving it a unique flavour, stronger than that of other game birds. It was a favourite of Queen Victoria and in the late nineteenth century many grand houses throughout Great Britain and Ireland had this recipe served on 12 August to celebrate the start of the shooting season.

This version is taken from my *Ultimate Game Cookbook*, published by Piatkus.

Serves 4

50 g/2 oz butter
juice of 1 lemon
225 g/8 oz redcurrants or cranberries
salt
freshly milled black pepper
4 oven-ready grouse
8 rashers of Ayrshire streaky bacon
chopped fresh thyme
50 g/2 oz beef dripping
2 slices of bread, cut into triangles

Preheat the oven to 200°C/400°F/Gas Mark 6.

Heat the butter in a saucepan, add the lemon juice and the redcurrants or cranberries with a sprinkling of salt and pepper, and cook for 1 minute. Allow to cool.

Fill the cavity of each grouse with the fruit mixture, seasoning the birds all over. Lay 2 slices of streaky bacon over each breast. Sprinkle with thyme.

Wrap the birds in some greased foil and place them breast down in a roasting tin. Cook for 15 minutes, remove the foil and roast for a further 10 minutes.

Heat the dripping in a frying pan and fry the bread triangles on both sides until golden brown.

Arrange the triangles on a large serving plate and sit the grouse on top of them. Serve with a Macallan Fine Oak 12-year-old whisky.

meat

For centuries, Scotland has enjoyed an unparalleled reputation for producing high-quality beef, lamb and pork, recognised as the crème de la crème of meat, eagerly sought after by leading chefs and consumers alike throughout the UK and Europe.

This reputation for quality is founded on the dedication, knowledge, and breeding and husbandry skills of specialist livestock producers. The outstanding meat is produced naturally in Scotland's beautiful countryside with the heather-filled hills and lush green fields where cattle and lambs roam freely.

orkney beef stew and dumplings

Another national institution. Having beef stew without dumplings would be like having roast beef without Yorkshire pudding – I just could not face life! Every town and village throughout Great Britain has its own version of beef stew; this is one of those really old village recipes from yesteryear.

Serves 4

900 g/2 lb Orkney shin beef, fat and gristle removed and diced
50 g/2 oz flour, well seasoned
50 g/2 oz beef dripping
2 onions, peeled and sliced
600 ml/1 pt beef stock (see p. 14)
150 ml/⅓ pt stout
salt
freshly milled black pepper
2 large potatoes, peeled and diced
1 large carrot, peeled and diced
175 g/6 oz button mushrooms, sliced
175 g/6 oz peas

FOR THE DUMPLINGS:
175 g/6 oz self-raising flour
pinch salt
freshly ground white pepper
75 g/3 oz beef suet
pinch fresh thyme

Toss the meat in the seasoned flour, heat the dripping in a large saucepan and fry the beef and onions for 5 minutes. Add the beef stock and stout, seasoning well with salt and pepper.

Bring the contents to the boil and remove any scum floating on the surface. Add the rest of the ingredients except the dumplings and stew slowly for 2 hours.

Meanwhile, make the dumplings. Mix the flour, salt and pepper in a bowl, stir in the suet and thyme and add just enough water to make a soft but not too sticky dough. Shape into 8 generous dumplings.

Add the dumplings and cook for a further 30 minutes. Serve this with a glass of cider.

aberdeen angus sirloin of scottish beef roasted with a herb crust and arran mustard yorkshire pudding

My Arran mustard Yorkshire puds are the talk of the isles. Visiting Arran is a wonderful experience. I had lunch at the Lagg Inn, which was built just before I was born, in 1791 – and I do know they were serving this roast beef then!

Serves 4

50 g/2 oz beef dripping
1.5 kg/3 lb sirloin of Aberdeen Angus beef
75 g/3 oz breadcrumbs
2 tsp mixed herbs
pinch madras curry powder

FOR THE YORKSHIRE PUDDING:
200 g/8 oz plain flour
pinch salt
2 large free-range eggs
400 ml/14 fl. oz fresh milk
200 ml/7 fl. oz cold water
2 tbsp of Arran mustard
50 g/2 oz beef dripping

Preheat the oven to 180°C/350°F/Gas Mark 4.

Trim the excess fat from the beef and cut small slits in the skin – this will allow the flavours from the herb crust to permeate the meat. Melt the dripping in a shallow baking tin and place the beef in it. Mix the rest of the ingredients in a bowl. Cover the top of the sirloin with this mixture, then roast in the oven for 70 minutes.

Meanwhile, make the pudding batter. Mix the flour and a pinch of salt into a bowl, then make a well in the centre and break in the eggs. Add half the milk and, using a wooden spoon, work it into the flour to form a paste, beating the mixture until it is smooth. Slowly add the rest of the milk and then the water, beating until the consistency is smooth. Whisk in the mustard.

Increase the oven temperature to 220°C/425°F/Gas Mark 8. Put the dripping into a large, deep baking tray and place in the oven for 3 minutes until the dripping is smoking. Pour in the mustardy Yorkshire batter and bake for 30 minutes.

Remove both the meat and the Yorkshire pudding. While the beef is resting for 25 minutes, make gravy with the beef juices: pour them into a pan and thicken slightly by adding a little cornflour and stirring over a low heat for a few minutes. Carve the beef and serve with the gravy and mustard Yorkshire pudding.

classic scotch beef and haggis in puff pastry

I devised this recipe for a Taste of Scotland cookery demonstration at the BBC Good Food Show at the NEC. It is now served at the Living Room restaurants in Edinburgh and Glasgow.

Serves 6–8

900 g/2 lb fillet of Aberdeen Angus beef
75 g/3 oz butter
2 large red onions, finely chopped
175 g/6 oz wild mushrooms
450 g/1 lb puff pastry (bought or see p. 144)
175 g/6 oz haggis
1 free-range egg, lightly beaten
salt
freshly milled black pepper

With a sharp knife, trim the fat from the beef fillet. Season the meat well with salt and pepper. Melt the butter in a large frying pan; add the beef, sealing the meat all over, cooking for at least 6 minutes. Remove the fillet from the pan, placing it to one side to cool.

In the same pan, add a little more butter and the chopped onion and mushrooms, cooking until all the moisture has evaporated. Season them well and allow them to cool.

Set the oven to 200°C/400°F/Gas Mark 6.

Roll out the pastry into a large rectangle and place on a greased baking tray.

Spread the onion and mushroom mixture onto the centre of the pastry, place the beef onto the mixture. Top the fillet with a layer of haggis.

Brush the edges of the pastry with the beaten egg, fold the pastry over, pressing the edges to seal it. Make some flowers and leaves from the leftover pastry to put on top and brush the whole thing with the rest of the beaten egg.

Bake in the centre of the oven for 20 minutes and then lower the oven to 180°C/350°F/Gas Mark 4 for a further 15 minutes until the pastry is golden brown.

Let the beef rest for 5 minutes before carving. Serve with Madeira sauce (see p. 24).

rare roast rib-eye of beef
with horseradish mash
and sweet potato crisps

A Cameron House speciality.

To roast a rib-eye of beef rare, allow 10 to 15 minutes per 450 g/1 lb; for medium, 20 minutes; and for well done, 25 minutes.

Serves 4

50 g/2 oz beef dripping
2.5 kg/5 lb rib-eye of Scottish beef
salt
freshly milled black pepper
thyme
sprigs of flat parsley

FOR THE SWEET POTATO CRISPS:
I sweet potato, peeled and thinly sliced
oil for deep-frying

FOR THE HORSERADISH MASH:
450 g/I lb of hot mashed potato
3 tbsp of creamed horseradish
30 g/I oz butter
salt
freshly milled black pepper

Preheat the oven to 190°C/375°F/Gas Mark 5.

Heat the dripping in a roasting pan and brown the joint all over. Place a wire rack on the roasting pan; place the beef on the rack. Season generously with salt and pepper, sprinkle with thyme and place in the centre of the oven for 75 minutes.

Meanwhile, deep-fry the sweet potato slices until they are crisp and golden.

Make up the hot mashed potato; add the creamed horseradish, butter, salt and pepper. Blend thoroughly.

Allow the beef to rest for at least 10 minutes before carving. Place a generous ball of mash on each warm plate with 2 slices of rare beef. Top the beef with the sweet potato crisps and the sprigs of parsley. Serve with fresh green beans and a little butter.

toad in the hole with aberdeen angus and ayrshire pork sausages

Toad in the hole today is like a national institution. One hundred and fifty years ago, beef, chicken, goat and even fish, rather than the great British banger, were used for this classic recipe. My preference is for a good Aberdeen Angus beef sausage and Ramsay's Ayrshire pork sausage. It is far better to make the batter the day before and let it settle in the fridge. I noticed while shopping at Tesco that they have placed Aberdeen Angus beef sausages in their 'Finest' range of foods, making these sausages more accessible throughout the UK.

Serves 4

450 g/1 lb Aberdeen Angus beef sausages
450 g/1 lb Ayrshire pork sausages
50 g/2 oz beef dripping

FOR THE YORKSHIRE PUDDING:
200 g/8 oz plain flour
pinch salt
2 large free-range eggs
400 ml/14 fl. oz fresh milk
200 ml/7 fl. oz cold water

Preheat the oven to 220°C/425°F/Gas Mark 8.

Place the pricked sausages in a large, deep baking tray with the dripping and bake for 10 to 12 minutes.

Meanwhile, make the batter. Mix the flour and a pinch of salt into a bowl, then make a well in the centre and break in the eggs. Add half the milk and, using a wooden spoon, work it into the flour to form a paste, beating the mixture until it is smooth. Slowly add the rest of the milk and then the water, beating until the consistency is smooth.

Carefully remove the hot tray from the oven, pour the batter over the sausages and return the tray to the oven for 30 minutes, until the batter is risen and golden brown.

Serve with the onion gravy on p. 23.

victorian pot-roasted beef
with horseradish sauce

In days of old when knights were bold and cookers hadn't been invented
They dug a hole in the middle of the ground and cooked, their hearts contented.

This very ancient dish is one of those that were copied by every cook and chef from the early fourteenth century onwards; Queen Victoria's chef, Charles Elme Francatelli, claimed this to be his own recipe! In 1862, he called it Braised Beef à la Polonaise aux Choux Rouges.

My version is a little modernised but the flavours and method are still Victorian. It is a regular feature at my dinner table, an excellent winter warmer that can be seen in many a household throughout the Highlands and Lowlands.

Serves 4

FOR THE HORSERADISH SAUCE:
150 ml/¼ pt of extra-thick double cream
5 tbsp freshly grated horseradish
1 tbsp wine vinegar
2 tsp English mustard
salt
freshly ground white pepper

1.8 kg/4 lb topside of Scottish beef
50 g/2 oz butter
20 shallots, peeled

4 large potatoes, peeled and quartered
2 large carrots, peeled and cut into chunks
2 parsnips, peeled and cut into chunks
1 small turnip, peeled and chopped
1 sprig of thyme
1 sprig of rosemary
salt
freshly milled black pepper
300 ml/½ pt beef stock (see p. 14)
150 ml/¼ pt of good-quality red wine (not plonk)

To make the horseradish sauce, lightly whip the cream and add all the rest of the ingredients, blending thoroughly. Place in the fridge until required.

Quickly fry the beef in the butter, browning it well all over, then place to one side. Fry the shallots, potatoes, carrot, parsnip and turnip in the butter and beef juices for about 6 minutes. Then place the beef, surrounded by the vegetables, in a large deep casserole or pot. Add the herbs, stock and wine, and season with salt and pepper.

Cover with a lid or cooking foil and place in the centre of the oven to cook for 2 hours. Half an hour before the meat is cooked, remove the lid or foil to allow the meat to brown a little more.

Let the meat rest for at least 15 minutes, then carefully slice it and place it with the vegetables on a large serving dish. Remove the thyme and rosemary sprigs and bring the stock juices to the boil. Add the cornflour blended with a little wine. Simmer for 4 minutes then pour around the vegetables. Serve with the horseradish sauce, garnished with fresh thyme.

braised oxtails

This really is food from the hearth of Scotland. I have been making this recipe for over 35 years and braised oxtails are still one of the dishes that I am most frequently asked to write about or demonstrate for television. Your butcher will trim and cut them for you. When buying oxtails, look for the short fat tails with a good proportion of meat on them. You will require a deep oven-to-table braising dish with a lid. The only way to eat oxtail is with your fingers, using a soup spoon for the gravy and a thick cottage loaf for dipping. Warm hand towels will be requested.

Serves 4

2 large oxtails (approx. 2 kg), cut and trimmed	salt
highly seasoned flour	freshly milled black pepper
40 g/1½ oz beef dripping	1 tbsp tomato purée
350 g/12 oz diced carrot	1 tbsp mushroom ketchup
350 g/12 oz chopped red onion	1 tbsp Worcestershire sauce
350 g/12 oz diced potato	1 tbsp lemon juice
150 ml/¼ pt of red wine	
570 ml/1 pt beef stock (see p. 14)	
1 sprig thyme	

Preheat the oven to 150°C/300°F/Gas Mark 2.

Trim any excess fat from the oxtails and toss them in the seasoned flour. Melt the beef dripping in a large saucepan. Add the oxtails a few pieces at a time and brown them all over. Place the browned oxtails to one side in a deep braising or casserole dish with a lid.

In the same pan, add the vegetables and brown them, cooking for about 4 minutes. Add the wine, stock, thyme and seasoning. Bring to the boil. Place the oxtails back in the pan and simmer on a low heat for 1 hour.

Place the meat and vegetables in the braising dish. Skim off any fat or scum from the saucepan and add the tomato purée, mushroom ketchup, Worcestershire sauce and lemon juice, and bring quickly to the boil. Simmer for 5 minutes until the flavours infuse and then pour over the oxtails and vegetables.

Cover the braising dish and place in the centre of the oven for 3 hours.

Remove the lid and allow the oxtails to stand for 10 minutes before serving. Serve with vegetable bubble and squeak cakes, for which a recipe is given on p. 49.

grilled sirloin steaks with arran mustard

I can remember the first time I tasted Arran mustard; I was working in Ayr, a young thin chef then! I went to the local, which was Kirkton Jean's Hotel in Kirkoswald, for a pint. (It is rumoured that the kirkyard in Kirkoswald is the site of Robert the Bruce's baptism.) The medium-rare grilled Scottish sirloin coated with Arran mustard on oatmeal bread was the number one bestselling sandwich in Kirkoswald, with poached Tayside salmon being the second most popular dish of the day.

You can use fillet of Ayrshire pork or fillet of lamb for this recipe, should you wish to do so, but a good sirloin of beef cannot be beaten.

Serves 4

4 x 225 g/8 oz sirloin steaks
75 g/3 oz Arran mustard
salt
freshly milled black pepper

Generously coat the steaks with the mustard, season well and grill for 5 to 15 minutes, turning them frequently, until they are cooked to your liking.

Serve on toasted wholemeal bread with a crisp summer red onion salad.

scotch collops

I created this recipe for a major food magazine which I was writing for in the 1980s. It is one of those recipes that improves if left to stand in its sauce and served the following day.

Serves 4

8 x 125 g/4 oz Scotch veal escalopes
50 g/2 oz butter
1 large red onion, finely chopped
175 ml/6 fl. oz dry white wine
400 ml/14 fl. oz chicken stock (see p. 15)
1 tbsp mushroom ketchup
2 tsp lemon juice
1 level tbsp plain flour
salt
freshly milled black pepper
pinch ground mace

Flatten the veal with a rolling pin. Melt half of the butter in a large frying pan, add the veal and cook for 3 minutes either side. Place the veal on a warm serving dish.

Add the onion to the frying pan and cook for 3 minutes. Pour in the wine and reduce by half. Add the chicken stock, mushroom ketchup and lemon juice. Bring to the boil and reduce again by half.

Mix together the flour and remaining butter. Add to the pan and whisk thoroughly until the sauce thickens. Season well with salt, pepper and a generous pinch of mace.

Spoon the sauce over the collops and serve with clapshot (see p. 57).

stoved chicken

This recipe uses a very similar method to the lamb dish Lancashire hot pot; even though I am a Lancashire lad, I do prefer this recipe using chicken.

Serves 4

50 g/2 oz butter
I tbsp vegetable oil
8 joints (about 900 g/2 lb) of chicken
225 g/8 oz lean rindless Ayrshire back bacon
salt
freshly milled black pepper
2 or 3 large onions, sliced
25 g/I oz plain flour
600 ml/I pt chicken stock (see p. 15)
2 tsp chopped fresh thyme
900 g/2 lb potatoes, peeled and thinly sliced
75 g/3 oz Scottish cheddar
50 g/2 oz oatmeal

Preheat the oven to 150°C/300°F/Gas Mark 2.

Heat the butter and oil in a large frying pan and quickly brown the chicken and bacon, cooking for about 5 minutes.

Remove the chicken and bacon to a large ovenproof casserole, season well and keep them warm in the oven.

Fry the onions until they become transparent, about 3 minutes. Add the flour and cook for 2 minutes; slowly add the chicken stock and season well, stirring all the time.

Remove the chicken and bacon from the oven and from the casserole dish. Sprinkle with the thyme and rearrange in the casserole dish, topping each layer of meat with a layer of potatoes. Finish with a layer of potatoes.

Pour over the onion and stock, and cover with a tight-fitting lid. Cook in the centre of the oven for 2 hours.

Remove the lid 20 minutes before the dish is ready, mix together the cheese and oatmeal and sprinkle them over the top to create a lovely crispy topping.

skirlie-stuffed chicken

I first tasted this about 30 years ago at the 'Gateway to Argyll and the Isles', the Caledonian Hotel at Station Square in Oban; I have yet to pay it another visit but I will do so.

This recipe is excellent made into sandwiches on crusty bread, although the oatmeal stuffing (the skirlie) is very filling. I add chicken stock to the skirlie so that it does not come out too dry. You can use dried herbs here but fresh ones are preferable.

Serves 4

1 large oven-ready free-range chicken
butter
salt
freshly milled black pepper

FOR THE SKIRLIE:
100 g/4 oz medium oatmeal
1 large onion, chopped
50 g/2 oz shredded beef suet
1 tsp finely chopped fresh thyme
1 tsp finely chopped fresh sage
1 tsp finely chopped fresh rosemary
100 ml/3 fl. oz chicken stock (see p. 15)

Preheat the oven to 200°C/400°F/Gas Mark 6.

Place all the dry skirlie ingredients into a large bowl and season them well, add the chicken stock and blend thoroughly. Place the mixture in the cavity of the chicken, put the chicken in a roasting tin and coat generously with butter and season with salt and pepper.

Place in the bottom of the oven and cook for about 90 minutes, basting every 20 minutes with the butter and juices from the chicken.

Place the chicken on a large serving dish and carve, making sure everyone gets plenty of the skirlie stuffing.

crown of orkney lamb

My wife Jayne and I had just returned from Porto Banus, Marbella. We had wined and dined the month away but I did miss my favourite meats, particularly traditional lamb roasts and stews. With lamb in abundance in the UK, it is without doubt one of the most popular meats in the British cookery calendar.

One of my favourite recipes is crown of Orkney lamb, which is rarely seen in restaurants or even supermarkets today. I like trying different versions of this classic dish. I still feel that my crown of lamb is the best of the many recipes that I have tried and tasted. You can make up the crown following the instructions below but I am sure your local butcher would do it for you.

Serves 4

2 best end necks of Orkney lamb, with 6 cutlets, trimmed
1 tbsp butter
1 onion, finely chopped
1 tsp fresh rosemary, ground in a pestle and mortar
1 eating apple, cored and chopped
1 pear, cored and chopped
100 g/4 oz fresh breadcrumbs
2 tbsp fresh chopped mint
1 free-range egg
salt
freshly milled black pepper
3 tbsp clear honey

Preheat the oven to 180°C/350°F/Gas Mark 4.

Trim each cutlet bone to a depth of 2.5 cm/1 in. with a sharp knife. Bend the joints around, fat side inwards, to form a crown. Cover each exposed bone with cooking foil and place on a small roasting tin.

Slowly melt the butter in a saucepan, add the onion, rosemary, apple and pear, and cook for 4 minutes. Add the breadcrumbs, mint and egg, and season well.

Fill the centre of the crown with the stuffing. Cover the crown with cooking foil and bake for 80 minutes.

Ten minutes before the end of the cooking time, remove the foil from the meat, leaving the bones covered, and pour the honey over the sides of the crown, avoiding the stuffing. Continue the cooking process. Remove all the foil and let the crown rest for at least 10 minutes before carving.

Serve with new potatoes and sugar peas.

lightly roasted rack of lamb

This is a really nice summer recipe and would make an ideal late supper served with rice or young vegetables.

Serves 4

1 or 2 racks of lamb, trimmed
25 g/1 oz butter
1 tbsp beef dripping
2 red onions, cut into wedges
1 red and 1 yellow pepper, cut into wedges
1 large courgette, sliced
1 sprig of mint, finely chopped
pinch nutmeg
salt
freshly milled black pepper

Preheat the oven to 150°C/300°F/Gas Mark 2.

Melt the butter in a frying pan and brown the rack of lamb all over, cooking for about 3 minutes.

Heat the dripping in a large casserole and place the lamb in it with the red onion, peppers, courgette, mint and nutmeg. Season well with salt and pepper and cook in the centre of the oven for 45 minutes.

Slice the rack into evenly sized cutlets and arrange them on a warm plate with buttered rice and vegetables.

SUSAN GIBSON ON SCOTTISH LAMB

Sue and Michael Gibson own Macbeth's of Forres and sell some of the finest produce in Scotland. I met Mike when I was writing my *Bridge Over Britain* and *Bridge on British Beef* cookbooks several years ago.

This is what Sue had to say about their lamb: 'Scotland is almost as well known for its lamb as its beef and the Moray hill farms have a high reputation for their ready supply of top-quality product. Most lamb is bred from Blackface and Cheviot ewes crossed with the Suffolk and fed on grass or heather in the summer, supplemented usually with some turnips or kale during the winter. Given our location, 'new season's' lamb is not usually available until July but the quality is then excellent right up until the New Year. Between January and June, the meat tends to have a stronger flavour more akin to mutton and we find that this appeals to many of our customers.'

slow-cooked gigot of lamb

Serves 4

1.8 kg/4 lb leg of lamb
100 g/4 oz dried yellow split peas, pre-soaked as instructed on
   packet
200 g/7 oz dried yellow lentils, pre-soaked as instructed on
  packet
300 ml/½ pt chicken stock (see p. 15)
1 bay leaf
1 tbsp honey, warmed
salt
freshly milled black pepper
450 g/1 lb buttery mashed potato with freshly chopped mint

FOR THE MARINADE:
300 ml/½ pt lamb stock
2 tbsp honey, warmed
1 tbsp garlic, crushed
1 tsp peppercorns, crushed
1 tbsp Worcestershire sauce
100 ml/3 fl. oz port
1 tbsp dried rosemary

Place the lamb in a deep casserole dish and cover with the
marinade ingredients. Blend the ingredients and lamb together well and chill in the fridge
for two days, mixing the ingredients and the lamb together three times a day.

Preheat the oven to 180°C/350°F/Gas Mark 4.

Braise the lamb slowly in the marinade for 3 hours.

Remove the lamb to a serving dish and keep warm. Strain the juices into a saucepan and
bring to the boil rapidly. Reduce the liquid by half.

Meanwhile, place the peas and lentils in a saucepan with the chicken stock and bay leaf,
bring to the boil and simmer for 30 minutes. Add the honey and season well.

Drain, remove the bay leaf and mash the peas and lentils with half of the mashed potato
and place on the base of a large, warmed serving plate.

Place the lamb in the centre and pour the sauce into a sauceboat. Garnish the dish with
sprigs of fresh mint and rosemary, and the rest of the mashed potato.

baked valentine lamb steaks with redcurrant sauce

Donald Russell (see Recommended Suppliers) sells heart-shaped cuts of lamb by mail order, or you could ask your butcher to cut the meat into heart shapes.

Serves 4

50 g/2 oz butter
4 x 285 g/10 oz Valentine lamb steaks, trimmed
1 large onion, diced
1 apple, peeled, cored and diced
225 g/8 oz redcurrants
25 g/1 oz butter
25 g/1 oz brown sugar
salt
freshly milled black pepper

Preheat the oven to 150°C/300°F/Gas Mark 2.

Melt the butter in a large frying pan and gently fry the steaks for 8 minutes either side. Remove the meat from the pan, place on a dish and keep warm in the oven.

In the same frying pan, fry the onions and apple together, browning the apple slightly. Add the redcurrants, butter and sugar, and cook gently for 4 minutes.

Remove 100 g/4 oz of the cooked redcurrants and reserve. Sieve the sauce and add the reserved cooked redcurrants to it.

Leave the steaks in the oven for 10 minutes.

Season them well with salt and pepper, garnish with the currant sauce and serve with snow peas and new potatoes.

oven-baked mini-loins of organic lamb with black cherry sauce

For this recipe, get your butcher to trim and tie four 250 g/8 oz boneless loins of lamb. For added flavour, I usually wrap them in naturally cured Ayrshire bacon and place a wooden cocktail stick through each one. This recipe only takes 30 minutes to make.

Serves 4

300 ml/½ pt lamb stock
3 tbsp port wine
300 ml/½ pt juice from tinned cherries
4 shallots, peeled and sliced
4 x 250 g/8 oz boneless loin of lamb
salt
freshly milled black pepper
50 g/2 oz beef dripping
pinch thyme

Preheat the oven to 220°C/425°F/Gas Mark 8.

Place the lamb stock, port, cherry sauce and sliced shallots in a saucepan and reduce by half.

Season the lamb on both sides. Add the cooking oil and the thyme to a griddle pan and heat. Cook the meat for 3 minutes on each side. Place the cherry sauce in a roasting tray, top with the lamb and bake in the centre of the oven for 15 minutes.

Remove the lamb and pour the sauce onto individual warm plates. Place two mini loins on each plate and garnish with vegetables of your choice.

breast of argyll lamb baked in heather honey with mint stuffing and rumbledethumps

Rumbledethumps come from the Borders and are a potato and cabbage dish very similar to colcannon. Make up the rumbledethumps during the lamb cooking process.

Serves 4

1.35 kg/3 lb breast of Argyll lamb
25 g/1 oz butter
1 large onion, finely chopped
1 free-range egg, beaten
30 ml/2 tbsp port
150 g/6 oz fresh breadcrumbs
1 tsp ground ginger
2 tbsp chopped parsley
1 tbsp fresh rosemary, chopped
4 tbsp finely chopped fresh mint
salt
freshly milled black pepper
2 tbsp of Scottish heather honey
sprigs fresh rosemary

FOR THE RUMBLEDETHUMPS:
450 g/1 lb cooked potato, roughly mashed
450 g/1 lb cooked spring cabbage, shredded
75 g/3 oz butter
6 spring onions, finely chopped
salt
freshly milled black pepper

Preheat the oven to 240°C/450°F/Gas Mark 9.

Melt the butter in a frying pan and fry the onion until soft.

In a separate bowl, beat the egg with the port and blend in the breadcrumbs, ginger, parsley, rosemary and mint. Add the onions and season the mixture with salt and pepper.

Flatten the meat and remove any excess fat. Place the mixture on the meat, then roll up the meat tightly and secure it with some butcher's string.

Place the lamb on a large piece of cooking foil. Warm the honey and pour over the lamb. Add the sprigs of fresh rosemary and secure the foil around the lamb so the honey and lamb juices do not escape.

Place in a roasting pan and cook in the oven for 40 to 50 minutes.

Very carefully remove the foil, retaining the juices and pouring them into a saucepan.

Return the meat to the oven for a further 15 minutes to brown.

Put some more finely chopped mint into the saucepan with the meat juices. Add 1 tablespoon of port, bring to the boil and let it simmer for 10 minutes, then strain the sauce through a fine sieve into a sauce boat and serve with the breast of lamb.

To make the rumbledethumps, place all the ingredients in a saucepan and reheat, blending them together. Add a little cream if desired. Taste and season.

slow-braised orkney organic lamb shanks in red wine sauce with mustard and mint mash

Having spent the past 30 years collecting, demonstrating and writing on the best of traditional British food for newspapers, magazines, radio and television, I was asked by *Life* magazine to share some of my favourite British recipes.

While pondering which ones to choose, I woke up one cold morning when it was wet and damp outside and I thought of comforting winter food. Scottish organic lamb shanks cooked properly really are one of the winter warmers to enjoy. This is a recipe I originally created for the *Richard & Judy* show early last year. It does take some time to cook but the best things in life are worth waiting for. In Scotland, Tony and Elizabeth Bown breed the finest organic meat I have ever tasted and they do mail order (see Orkney Organic Meat in Recommended Suppliers), so there is no excuse for not using the best ingredients. The vegetables do not need to be peeled and can be added whole or chopped.

Serves 4

600 ml/1 pt of fresh chicken stock (see p. 15)
1 bottle of good-quality red wine
50 g/2 oz duck fat
4–6 medium-size Orkney organic lamb
   shanks
2 large carrots
2 large red onions
1 garlic bulb
3 sprigs rosemary
salt

freshly milled black pepper
25 g/1 oz butter

FOR THE MASH:
450 g/1 lb mashed potato
35 g/1½ oz butter
3 tbsp cream
1 tbsp English mustard
1 tbsp fresh mint, chopped
salt
freshly milled black pepper

Preheat the oven to 300°C/150°F/Gas Mark 2.

First, mix the chicken stock with a good-quality red wine.

Into a large pot or pan add the duck fat, the lamb shanks, the vegetables and herbs, and cook, stirring, for a good 20 minutes. Pour in the wine and stock, and season with salt and pepper, then place in the oven for 3 hours, stirring every 30 minutes.

Allow the meat and stock to rest for 2 hours. Remove the shanks with a slotted spoon. Remove the meat from the bones; it should come away very easily.

Make the mashed potato, adding the butter, cream, mustard and mint. Season well and place to one side. Place the mash on a serving dish, top with the shanks and place in a warm oven.

Strain the cooking liquid through a fine sieve into a saucepan and bring to the boil. Reduce by half, add the butter and pour over the shanks.

Serve with fresh crusty bread and some more red wine.

roast lamb with rosemary, cinnamon and honey sauce

The flavours of the cinnamon and honey make this festive – a great alternative to turkey during the season of goodwill to all who love food.

Serves 4–6

1. 35 kg/3 lb leg of lamb, boned and rolled
salt
freshly milled black pepper
2 cloves garlic, crushed
1 tsp paprika

FOR THE SAUCE:
3 sprigs fresh rosemary soaked in 6 tbsp fresh orange juice
6 tbsp clear honey
1 tsp cinnamon
1 tbsp chopped fresh mint
150 ml/5 fl. oz beef stock (see p. 14)
1 tbsp cornflour mixed with a little orange juice

Preheat the oven to 200°C/400°F/Gas Mark 6.

Rub the lamb with the salt, pepper, garlic and paprika and cook in the oven for 30 minutes.

Meanwhile, place the rest of the ingredients except the cornflour in a saucepan and bring to the boil, then simmer for 15 minutes. Add the cornflour and cook over a low heat for a few minutes, stirring, to thicken.

Baste the meat with the rosemary and honey sauce every 15 minutes for 1 hour.

Remove the lamb to a large serving plate and carve; add the juices to the rest of the rosemary and honey sauce, heat for a minute or two.

Serve with the sauce, new potatoes and fresh winter cabbage.

jacqueline's roast loin of ayrshire pork with sage and onion stuffing

Ramsay of Carluke are the best producers of pork in Scotland. They are based in the Clyde Valley in Lanarkshire, a lovely part of the world with some beautiful scenery and historical attractions such as the fascinating model village New Lanark. If you happen to be in the area, the Ramsays' shop is well worth a visit (see Recommended Suppliers). This recipe is named after Jacqueline Ramsay, who runs the company with her husband Andrew.

It is important that you adhere to the cooking time of 30 minutes per 450 g/1 lb. Serves 4–6

900 g–2.5 kg/2 lb–6 lb high-quality loin of pork	FOR THE STUFFING:
fresh rosemary	225 g/8 oz good-quality pork sausage meat
bay leaves	15 g/3 oz fresh white breadcrumbs
coarse salt	1 small onion finely chopped
freshly milled black pepper	1 tbsp dried sage
2 tbsp Scottish heather honey	1 tbsp melted butter
	salt
	freshly milled black pepper
	4 tbsp chicken stock (see p. 15)

Preheat the oven to 240°C/450°F/Gas Mark 9.

Take the loin of pork and carefully score the skin and a little of the fat below it with a *very* sharp knife, making criss-crossing cuts about 1 cm/½ in. apart. Gently brush the pork with a little oil and salt the skin generously all over.

To get the crackling really crisp, place the joint skin side down in a roasting tray and pour in about 2.5 cm/1 in. of boiling water.

Place the tray in the centre of the oven and cook for 20 minutes.

Remove the tray, set the pork to one side and pour off the liquid, which will be used for basting the pork.

Place the pork back in the roasting tin, skin side up. Season and add a few bay leaves and some rosemary into the score marks.

Reduce the heat to 180°C/350°F/Gas Mark 4.

Cook for 30 minutes to the pound, basting every 20 minutes.

To make the stuffing, simply mix all the ingredients together well in a bowl and then turn out into a greased ovenproof dish. Place in the oven with the pork for the last 35 minutes' cooking time.

Allow the joint to cool and then remove the crackling. Cut into long thin strips and place on a baking tray. Salt, coat with the heather honey, and cook for a further 10 minutes.

Slice and arrange the pork and crackling in a fanned circle. Serve hot or cold, with apple sauce.

fillet of ayrshire pork in cream sauce with prunes

A popular lunch dish in my house, gob-smacking good.

Serves 4

1 kg/2 lb Ayrshire pork, diced
freshly milled black pepper
freshly grated nutmeg
50 g/2 oz butter
8 shallots, peeled and sliced
75 g/3 oz celery, thinly sliced
225 g/8 oz prunes, stones removed
salt
2 tbsp chicken stock (see p. 15)
300 ml/½ pt sour cream

Season the diced pork fillet well with black pepper and nutmeg.

Heat the butter in a large frying pan and cook the shallots and celery for 4 minutes. Add the pork and cook for a further 15 minutes, then add the prunes and cook for another 2 minutes. Season with salt and a little more nutmeg, add the chicken stock and sour cream and cook for 1 minute. Serve with clapshot (see p. 57).

fish

On the west coast of Scotland, you will find hundreds of small spate rivers, streams and lochs, while in the east you find the famous fishing rivers the Tay, Tweed and Dee, and the classic salmon river, the Spey. This river possesses a fishing mythology unlike any other and has lured some of the world's best fishermen, who come seeking the elusive salmon. Further north is Caithness and Sutherland, which is a patchwork quilt of lochs, streams and rivers. Exceptional fishing can be found throughout, even on the small islands. To the south, closer to the border with England, there is the Tweed on the east coast, known for its salmon, and to the west, the Solway rivers which are famous for their sea trout as well as running salmon. It is no wonder that fish from around Scotland is sought after by gourmets and that fishing and fish restaurants attract visitors to Scotland from all over the world.

One of my favourite fish indigenous to Scotland is the brown trout, with its brown-black flecked skin and light pink flesh; the flavour when cooked is exceptional. The most important thing to remember is that the fish must be extremely fresh. When I buy salmon or brown trout, the first thing I look for is that the gills are moist and red, not grey. The eyes should be bright and stand out; if they are dull and sunken, then the fish is not fresh. The body should be firm to the touch and not slimy, and there should be almost no smell. Try to buy from a reputable fishmonger or companies like Loch Fyne Oysters and Salar Salmon. Have a look at the Recommended Suppliers section at the back of the book for inspiration.

to pickle mackrel, called caveach

Cured fish has been part of Scottish heritage for centuries. The most popular are smoked salmon, trout and my special favourite Arbroath smokies, which I serve on potato cakes and use in fish soups and for pâtés.

This recipe is a traditional way of preserving fish, from a book of recipes collected by 'a Gentlewoman who formerly kept a Boarding School'. Today, you can buy pickled herrings in any supermarket, but ensure the word 'Scottish' comes into play.

Cut your Mackrel into round Pieces, and divide one into five or six Pieces:
To fix large Mackrel you may take one Ounce of Beaten Pepper, three large Nutmegs, a little Mace, and a Handful of Salt; mix your Salt and beaten spice together, and make two or three Holes in each Piece, and thrust the Seasoning into those Holes with your Fingers; rub the Pieces all over with the seasoning; fry them brown in Oil, and let them stand till they dry; then put them into Vinegar, and cover them with Oil. They will keep well covered a great while, and are very delicious.

The Lady's Companion, 1733

herrings in oatmeal

Wha'll buy my caller herrin'?
They're bonnie fish and dainty farin'.
Wha'll buy my caller herrin'
New drawn frae the Forth?

Lady Nairne

This is a classic recipe of Scotland, one of the simplest and yet good for the body and soul. I think Tilquhillie oats are the best – they can be purchased at Jenners and Harvey Nichols or direct from the company (see Recommended Suppliers).

It is far easier to make this recipe today than it once would have been because herrings can be bought already filleted. In the 1920s, when it was at the height of its popularity, you would have had to gut and fillet the herrings yourself; today you can buy them direct from the Orkney Herring Company in Stromness. You can use any oily fish, such as brown trout or mackerel, for this recipe. If you can, save the fat from grilled bacon or roast pork to use here where dripping is called for, as they will add extra flavour.

Serves 4

6–8 raw herring fillets
50 g/2 oz seasoned flour
1 free-range egg, beaten with a little milk
100 g/4 oz Tilquhillie oatmeal
100 g/4 oz dripping
1 tbsp sunflower oil
25 g/1 oz butter
2 lemons

Lightly coat the herrings in the seasoned flour then dip them into the egg mixture; finally, coat them with the oatmeal.

Heat the dripping, sunflower oil and butter in a large frying pan and, when the fat is sizzling, fry the herrings for about 2 minutes on each side.

Sit the herrings on a warm serving dish and sprinkle with freshly squeezed lemon juice. Dress with slices of lemon and serve with a healthy herb salad.

devilled orkney hele sild

Orkney hele sild is a type of small, sardine-like fish, quite hard to get hold of in Britain, but very popular in Scandinavia. It is usually served in a potato basket, garnished with prawns and a sprinkling of cayenne pepper, hence 'devilled'. It is often accompanied with triangles of fried bread dipped in chopped parsley.

Hele sild can be ordered from the Orkney Herring Company (see Recommended Suppliers) but you could use whitebait, sardines or herrings for this recipe.

Serves 4

300 ml/½ pt fresh milk
450 g/1 lb fresh hele sild
100 g/4 oz plain white flour
1 tsp salt
1 tsp cayenne pepper
freshly milled black pepper
cooking oil, for deep-frying

FOR THE GARNISH:
cayenne
2 lemons, sliced
sprigs of fresh mint

Pour the milk into a bowl and soak the fish in the milk for about 15 minutes.

Meanwhile, put the flour, salt, cayenne and a little black pepper into a plastic bag and shake well.

Drain the sild, being very careful not to break them.

Place the flour mixture on a large, deep plate and gently toss the fish in the flour, again being very careful not to break them.

Heat a deep frying pan half-filled with cooking oil to about 190°C/375°F. The oil should sizzle when you test it by dropping in one of the sild.

Add about half the fish first, deep-frying them for about 5 minutes until they are very crisp and golden brown.

Sit them on some kitchen paper to drain and keep them warm. Repeat the process with the rest of the fish.

Serve sprinkled with cayenne pepper and garnished with lemon slices and sprigs of fresh mint.

marinated kipper fillets

The curers at Loch Fyne in Scotland are modern-day masters of their trade but the first kippers were actually prepared in the 1840s at the sea houses – huts on the shore where the fishwives worked, gutting and cleaning the fish fresh from the boats – in Northumberland.

Some people like their kippers grilled or fried but this really is a great lunchtime snack and very healthy indeed.

Serves 4

3 pairs good-quality kipper fillets, uncooked

FOR THE MARINADE:
1 tbsp Arran mustard
1 clove of garlic, crushed
3 tbsp groundnut oil
2 tbsp tarragon vinegar
2 shallots, finely sliced
1 tbsp chopped fresh parsley
juice of 1 lemon
freshly milled black pepper

FOR THE GARNISH:
1 lemon, sliced
fresh parsley

Ensure that all bones are removed from the kippers.

Cut each fillet diagonally into 5 strips, following the natural grain.

Put all the marinade ingredients into a bowl and blend with a wooden spoon.

Place the fillets in the marinade, cover with clingfilm and place in the refrigerator for 24 hours.

Carefully remove the fillets from the marinade with a slotted spoon and place them on a serving dish, garnished with lemon and parsley. Pour over a little of the marinade and serve with rye bread and a fresh watercress salad.

potted salar smoked salmon

In the Lakes they make potted fish with trout or char, in Northern Ireland they use smoked mackerel, and the Welsh use herrings. But for a special occasion, there really is only one way to go and that is using Salar smoked salmon.

Eric and Jane Twelves own an incredible business called Salar Smokehouse in Lochcarnan on South Uist in the Outer Hebrides, where they cure their award-winning, flaky smoked salmon with skill and care. What can I say that Nick Nairn and my food hero Rick Stein have not already said? It is a unique flavour that every salmon-lover must try.

It is important not to use a blender for this recipe – remember it is the salmon that is the star.

Serves 4

350 g/12 oz Salar smoked salmon, flaked
generous pinch nutmeg
generous pinch mace
100 g/4 oz softened butter
salt
freshly milled black pepper
2 tbsp port or sherry
2 tbsp double cream
25 g/1 oz butter for the earthenware pots
1 lemon, thinly sliced
sprigs fresh parsley

Salar Smokehouse, Lochcarnan, South Uist

Remove the skin from the salmon, flaking it into a large bowl with all the ingredients except the lemon and parsley. Mix together thoroughly until very smooth.

Place the smoked salmon mixture into one large or several individual buttered earthenware pots.

Cover with buttered greaseproof paper and weigh the filling down with something heavy.

Leave in the refrigerator for at least 24 hours.

Remove the paper and dress the salmon with slices of fresh lemon and parsley.

Serve with slices of warm toast or oatcakes.

brown trout with naturally cured smoked bacon

I have a neighbour who goes fishing all the time and he brings me back some trout from nearly every trip. The flavour of wild trout is far superior to that of farmed. I love bacon and we have some of the finest curers on our doorstep. Ramsay's Ayrshire bacon is not injected with water and is naturally cured.

This makes an excellent barbecue recipe – just place the prepared fish in a barbecue basket. Serves 4

4 x 275 g/10 oz brown trout, gutted and cleaned
salt
freshly milled black pepper
2 apples, peeled, cored and sliced
4 sprigs fresh mint
juice of 1 lemon
12 rashers rindless smoked streaky bacon
25 g/1 oz butter

FOR THE GARNISH:
2 apples, cored and sliced
2 lemons, sliced
4 sprigs fresh mint

Preheat the oven to 200°C/400°F/Gas Mark 6.

Open up the cavity of each trout and wash thoroughly with warm salt water.

Season each cavity with salt and pepper, and place an equal amount of sliced apple into each fish with a sprig of mint.

Squeeze lemon juice over each cavity. Carefully wrap the whole of each trout except the head and tail with three rashers of smoked bacon.

Grease a deep baking tray with the butter and sit the trout in it with the loose ends of the bacon underneath. Season with pepper and bake for 20 minutes, turning the trout after 10 minutes.

Remove from the oven onto a serving dish and garnish with sliced apple, lemon and fresh mint.

LOCH FYNE OYSTERS

When Jayne and I are driving to Scotland, we always plan what we are going to do, where we are going to go and, most importantly, which restaurants we are going to visit. The one place we never fail to go is the Loch Fyne Oyster Bar at Cairndow. It is incredibly picturesque and only about a 40-minute drive from Loch Lomond. Jayne always has her priorities right, so I agree that Jayne drives there and I drive back. Why, you ask? She loves a glass of champagne with her fish and I can enjoy one small glass of the local beer. I always hope to be there when the specials board in the restaurant includes the battered fish that is so light it floats off the plate — somehow they seem to know when I am coming. (The recipe is on p. 135.)

When you come to the Oyster Bar, you think, this is tiny. Then you see the shop area bursting at the seams with a collection of the finest Scottish fish and seafood you are ever likely to encounter. As well as fish, they stock well-known names in game, meat, dairy and preserves. The staff at this family-owned firm are extremely friendly and are there to help you purchase exactly what you require. The beauty of the restaurant and shop being together is that you can go to the restaurant, taste the Loch Fyne produce and then go to the shop and buy it to take home to friends and family.

My shopping list is nearly always the same: I always buy, for the week's stay at our lodge on Loch Lomond, their Bradan Orach smoked salmon, for breakfast with scrambled eggs; Loch Fyne kippers; oysters, to go with champagne of course; sherry-pickled herrings for a light lunch; and Isle of Mull cheddar, smoked venison and Arran mustard for my Scottish ploughman's lunch with a bottle of their Fyne Ales Highlander beer. Now you can see why I like Scotland so much!

trompetto's oysters

Silvino Trompetto, Tromps, was my mentor and dear friend. Not only was he one of the most famous of the Savoy Hotel chefs but he was also one of the very first television chefs, along with Phillip Harben and Fanny Craddock, so it is not surprising that I created this recipe for him in 1982.

Caviar is of course optional! The Orkney Herring Company makes a marvellous Sea Relish containing seaweed extract which would be a truly delicious substitute.

Serves 4

3 dozen fresh oysters in their natural juices
50 g/2 oz butter, softened
50 g/2 oz plain flour
300 ml/½ pt dry white wine
2 shallots, finely chopped
1 tbsp finely chopped parsley
1 tsp anchovy essence
salt
freshly milled black pepper
175 g/6 oz white crab meat

75 g/3 oz creamy Scottish cheddar cheese, grated
75 g/3 oz Stilton cheese, crumbled
125 g/4 oz smoked salmon, chopped
175 g/6 oz fresh breadcrumbs
6 slices of bread
2 cloves garlic, crushed
50 g/2 oz butter
1 small jar of caviar (optional)
1 lemon, very thinly sliced

In a large sauté pan, poach the oysters in their juices for 4 minutes.

Strain the oyster liquid into a bowl and set aside.

Melt the butter in a saucepan. Add the flour and cook for 2 minutes, blending all the time. Add the white wine and shallots. Bring to the boil and add the reserved oyster juice. Let this reduce by a third, simmering for about 1 hour.

Preheat the oven to 200°C/400°F/Gas Mark 6.

Add the parsley and anchovy essence, season well and cook for a further 15 minutes. Remove the pan from the heat and carefully blend in the oysters and crab meat.

Spoon the mixture into individual ramekins. Mix together the two cheeses and the smoked salmon, and sprinkle over the oyster mixture, topping with breadcrumbs.

Bake in the oven for 10 minutes.

Meanwhile, cut the crusts off the bread, mix the garlic into the butter and fry the bread in the garlic butter until it is golden brown.

Serve the oysters straight from the oven in their ramekins, topping each dish with a little caviar and a slice of lemon, with the garlic fried bread on the side.

fresh oysters and champagne

In 2004, David Austin, wine buyer for the Balmoral Hotel in Edinburgh, was awarded the grand title of Champagne Academician. Each year, a select few from the UK are invited to Champagne for one week; at the end of this course, the candidates sit an exam and the successful ones join this elite club of champagne connoisseurs, also known as 'Old Boys' within the industry.

To celebrate this award, the Palm Court bar at the Balmoral served a glass of Dom Perignon, vintage 1996, with Loch Fyne oysters, which I had to have and thoroughly enjoyed – a reminder that the simple things in life are always the best.

Serves 2

2 dozen fresh oysters, opened, on ice
3 lemons, quartered
salt
freshly milled black pepper
1 bottle of your favourite champagne or white wine, chilled

Squeeze the lemons onto the oysters, season and enjoy with your favourite champagne or wine.

buttered scottish lobster

This is an old recipe and there have been many different versions over the years. The following one dates from 1767: 'Cut up the Lobster small. Put it into a stew pan with a little gravy, butter, pepper, salt and vinegar. Set it over the fire till hot. Heat the shells, and serve the lobsters in them.'

Mrs Rundell's 1846 book *A New System of Domestic Cookery* adds a little nutmeg, and flour to thicken. Patrick Lamb in his *Royal Cookery* (1710) recommends adding minced anchovy and covering the lobster with pastry.

Here's my version.

Serves 4

2 cooked lobsters, about 700 g/1½ lb each
zest and juice of 1 lemon
100 g/4 oz butter
4 tbsp fresh white breadcrumbs
2 tbsp brandy
5 tbsp double cream or crème fraîche
salt
freshly milled black pepper
50 g/2 oz Scottish cheddar cheese, grated
2 lemons, sliced
1 kiwi fruit, peeled and sliced
4 king prawns, shells on, cooked
sprigs fresh dill

Preheat oven to 160°C/325°F/Gas Mark 3.

Ask your fishmonger to remove the meat from the lobsters and keep the shells aside for you. Chop the meat and put it in a bowl. Add the lemon juice and zest.

Clean the shells thoroughly and place on a baking tray in the oven.

Fry the breadcrumbs in 25 g/1 oz of the butter until crisp and golden brown, about 3 minutes. Set aside.

Melt the remaining butter in a saucepan and gently heat the lobster meat. Add the brandy and cook for a further 3 minutes. Add the cream or crème fraîche, salt and pepper.

Place the buttered lobster into the shells, cover with the grated cheddar and the toasted breadcrumbs, and grill for a few minutes until golden brown.

Garnish with the slices of lemon and kiwi fruit, king prawns and sprigs of dill.

lobster tail summer salad

I love the taste of lobster tails blended with a summer salad and they are an excellent accompaniment to a rare grilled Aberdeen Angus rib-eye or a centre-cut fillet steak. I would recommend serving a bottle of Gorse wine from the Orkney Wine Company with this recipe. The wine is made from handpicked gorse flowers and complements the summery flavours of the salad perfectly.

Serves 6

450 g/1 lb cooked lobster-tail meat, sliced
175 g/6 oz shredded white cabbage
75 g/3 oz chopped celery
75 g/3 oz grated carrot
1 bunch spring onions, cleaned, ends removed, and chopped
2 whites of leeks, cleaned and chopped
3 beef tomatoes, chopped
1 apple, cored, peeled and diced
4 tbsp of virgin olive oil
1 tbsp chopped fresh basil
salt
freshly milled black pepper

Simply toss all the ingredients in a large salad bowl, season with salt and pepper and chill for 1 hour.

Garnish with a little chopped fresh basil and some whole leaves.

lobster sauce for fish

Several years ago, I wrote a book called *200 Classic Sauces* and of the 200, this is without doubt the most popular. It's expensive to make but well worth every pound, shilling and penny. It can be served with almost any seafood dish of your choice, hot or cold, but for the ultimate combination, try this with poached salmon or brown trout and a fresh herb salad. You can freeze this sauce.

2 lobsters, about 1 kg/2 lb each, uncooked	1 litre/1¾ pt fish stock (see p. 19)
75 g/3 oz butter	150 ml/¼ pt Madeira
100 g/4 oz shallots, finely chopped	150 ml/¼ pt single cream
50 g/2 oz celery, finely chopped	pink peppercorns
100 g/4 oz carrot, roughly chopped	freshly ground white pepper
4 tbsp brandy	salt
2 tbsp balsamic vinegar	bouquet garni
75 g/3 oz flour	150 ml/¼ pt double cream
4 tbsp tomato purée	

Ask your fishmonger to kill the lobsters and cut them in half for you, and to give you the shells and any spawn.

Melt the butter in a saucepan, adding all the pieces of lobster, the shallots, celery and carrot. Cook this slowly without colouring the butter for 4 minutes, stirring continuously with a wooden spoon. Add the brandy and set it on fire.

Add the balsamic vinegar and cook for a further 2 minutes, then remove from the heat and mix in the flour and tomato purée.

Return to the heat and cook gently, gradually adding the fish stock, Madeira, single cream and pink peppercorns.

Bring to the boil, stirring all the time, add the seasoning and bouquet garni, and simmer for at least 35 minutes.

Remove the lobster pieces and extract the meat from them.

Crush any lobster spawn you might have set aside earlier and blend it in to the sauce with the double cream. Reboil slowly for 5 minutes and strain.

When serving lobster sauce, I always top the sauce with lobster butter, which can be made quite easily: blend some crushed coral of lobster in a pestle and mortar with a bay leaf and a pinch of dried thyme. Then blend the ingredients with 4 tablespoons of softened butter and 2 finely chopped shallots which have been gently sautéd and then rubbed through a fine sieve.

Make the mixture into a sausage shape, wrap in foil and place in the freezer for 30 minutes. Slice very thinly onto the sauce, alternating with slices of lemon.

baked king scallops

I first tasted a recipe similar to this at The Witchery restaurant in Edinburgh. Their chef served it with a lobster sauce, which was yummy.

Serves 4

12 king scallops, in their shells
150 ml/⅓ pt fish stock (see p. 19)
1 onion, chopped
salt
freshly milled black pepper
zest and juice of 2 lemons
150 ml/⅓ pt double cream
200 g/8 oz cheddar cheese, grated

Preheat the oven to 180°C/350°F/Gas Mark 4.

To remove the scallops from their shells, scrape off the surrounding fringe (beard) and the black intestinal thread. The white part is the flesh and the orange part (coral) is the roe. Very carefully ease the flesh and coral from the shell with a short but very strong knife. Wash the shells thoroughly and dry them well. Place all 12 shells on a baking tray and set aside for later.

Put the scallops, fish stock and onion in an ovenproof baking dish, season, cover with cooking foil and bake for 8 minutes.

Remove the foil and return the scallops to their shells using a slotted spoon. Add 1 tablespoon of the fish-stock liquid to each shell, with a squeeze of lemon and a little double cream. Top each shell with some grated cheese.

Turn the heat up to 240°C/450°F/Gas Mark 9. Return the scallops to the oven for a further 4 minutes.

Serve with crusty brown bread and butter.

wild salmon and haddock fish cakes

The humble fish cake was once a quick, easy way to use up leftovers but since it has become fashionable, there have been a great many new versions, some of them delicious. One thing I don't agree with, though, is the recent tendency to make them smaller and smaller. A fish cake should look like what it is – a good, hearty snack – and not be the size of a 50-pence piece.

Serves 4

450 g/1 lb fresh salmon fillet, skin removed
450 g/1 lb fresh haddock fillet, skin removed
2 free-range eggs, beaten
450 g/1 lb mashed potato
175 g/6 oz breadcrumbs
50 ml/2 fl. oz double cream
50 ml/2 fl. oz lemon juice
salt
freshly milled black pepper
beef dripping

Flake or roughly chop the raw fish, checking that no bones remain. Add it to the rest of the ingredients except the dripping, blending them thoroughly and ensuring that they are well seasoned.

Shape the mixture into cakes about 3 cm/1 in. thick and about 8 cm/3 in. in diameter and place in the fridge for at least 4 hours until chilled.

Place the fish cakes into hot dripping and fry them for 4 to 5 minutes until golden brown on both sides. Drain them on kitchen paper and serve them with a homemade tartare sauce or, if you're feeling really flush, my lobster sauce (see p. 128).

scottish fish casserole

You can use any fish for this recipe. I like hake or cod with salmon for colour and flavour. Smoked mussels or oysters are a tasty addition, too. Do try to use wild salmon where possible.

Serves 4

450 g/1 lb salmon fillet, skinned and chopped
450 g/1 lb hake fillet, skinned and chopped
75 g/3 oz plain flour, seasoned
75 g/3 oz butter
4 shallots, skinned and finely chopped
1 carrot, peeled and diced
1 leek, washed and finely chopped
300 ml/½ pt dry white wine
300 ml/½ pt medium-sweet cider
2 tsp anchovy essence
1 tbsp tarragon vinegar
200 g/8 oz Loch Fyne smoked mussels (optional)

Coat the fish in 25g/1 oz of the seasoned flour.

Melt the butter in a flameproof casserole and add the fish, shallots, carrot and leek, cooking gently for 10 minutes. Sprinkle with the remaining flour, stirring for 2 minutes.

Slowly add the wine, cider, anchovy essence and tarragon vinegar.

Bring to the boil then turn the heat down and simmer for 35 minutes. Add the smoked mussels after 25 minutes, if using. Alternatively, you could bake the casserole in the oven for 30 minutes at 180°C/350°F/Gas Mark 4.

Sprinkle with freshly chopped parsley and serve with warm crusty brown bread.

casserole of naturally cured smoked haddock on a bed of mash with passion fruit and mustard sauce

This is a recipe with all the gusto of everything that's Scottish in the form of naturally cured smoked haddock, with the added flavour of my passion fruit and mustard sauce. Cod, monkfish or sole could all be substituted for haddock if you prefer. It is important, however, that if you do use haddock, you do not use the yellow dyed rubbish from the supermarket.

Serves 4

450 g/1 lb smoked haddock fillet, cut into
    4 slices
50 g/2 oz butter
600 ml/1 pt milk
450 g/1 lb mashed potato
25 g/1 oz plain flour
freshly milled black pepper
pinch freshly grated nutmeg
3 tbsp passion fruit pulp
1 tbsp Arran mustard
1 tbsp chopped parsley

Preheat the oven to 200°C/400°F/Gas Mark 6.

Make up the mashed potato and keep warm.

Use half of the butter to grease an ovenproof casserole. Put the haddock fillets into it, pour over the milk and cook for 15 minutes in the centre of the oven.

Carefully drain the milk and set aside, being very careful not to break the fish in the casserole.

Put a large spoonful of mash on each plate, top with a fillet of haddock and keep warm.

Melt the remaining butter in a saucepan and add the flour, stirring. Slowly whisk in the milk the fish was cooked in and season with the pepper and nutmeg. Stirring all the time, add the passion fruit, mustard and parsley, blending thoroughly.

Pour the sauce around the haddock and potato and serve immediately with fresh boiled beetroot.

pan-fried monkfish with rowanberries and a whisky and ginger cream sauce

I have to thank Simon Whitley at Cameron House, Loch Lomond, for this very unusual recipe – a true taste of Scotland.

Serves 4

75 g/3 oz fresh rowanberries
60 ml/2 fl. oz malt whisky
25 g/1 oz butter
3 tbsp olive oil
1 stalk lemongrass, finely sliced
675 g/1½ lb fresh monkfish tail fillets, skinned
75 g/3 oz stem ginger in syrup, sliced
salt
freshly milled black pepper
60 ml/2 fl. oz double cream
2 tbsp chopped fresh parsley
2 limes, thinly sliced

Soak the rowanberries in the whisky for 1 hour.

Heat the butter and olive oil in a large pan. Add the lemongrass and monkfish tails and cook for 4 minutes on each side, until golden brown.

Add the stem ginger and ginger syrup, rowanberries, whisky and seasoning.

Cook for a further 8 minutes. Add the cream and cook for a further 3 minutes, garnish with parsley and fresh lime slices.

haddock in loch fyne batter with fat chips

My wife Jayne and I had this recipe at the Loch Fyne restaurant during our last visit and the batter was so light, I had to ask for the recipe and was politely told, 'Figure it out, Tam.' Not really – they very kindly sent me the following batter recipe.

The chips must be big and chunky, and cooked with the fish in a good beef dripping, if possible, for that special homemade flavour.

For a more rustic batter, add 25 g/1 oz oatmeal to the batter.

Serves 6

6 x 225 g/8 oz haddock or cod fillets
1 kg/2 lb potatoes, peeled and chipped
dripping or sunflower oil for deep frying
salt
freshly ground white pepper

FOR THE BATTER:
340 g/12 oz plain flour
generous pinch white pepper
70 ml/2½ fl. oz olive oil
425 ml/¾ pt water with a pinch of salt dissolved in it
3 free-range eggs

To make the batter, sieve the flour with the pepper into a large bowl. Make a well in the centre of the flour. Pour a little oil into the well and mix it with the flour.

Gradually combine the olive oil with the flour, adding the water slowly at the same time. Beat the eggs and mix them into the batter. Leave to stand for 10 minutes.

Heat the oil until it gives off a faint, almost invisible blue smoke (180°C/350°F). Fry the chips in small batches. When they start to brown, remove them with a slotted spoon or if you use a basket, the basket. Keep them warm in the oven.

Season each piece of fish and then dip into the batter, drawing backwards and forwards 2 or 3 times to coat the fish fully.

Fry the fillets one at a time, lowering them gently into the hot fat, skin side down to prevent them from curling.

After 5 minutes turn the fish over, cooking for a further 3 minutes until golden brown.

Traditionally, fish and chips should be served on newspaper with salt and malt vinegar.

savoury pies and puddings

Having spent several years of my career working in the development of this wonderful product, I find it very hard to stop myself making the recipes tastier and tastier! The art of pie-making is quite simple: use fresh, high-quality ingredients – don't skimp and you will not be disappointed. I create at least one pie idea a month, experimenting on the taste buds of my family and friends.

In fact, I love pies so much that I even started my own Pie Society. For about 15 years now, my friends and I have got together in the week before Christmas. While our wives go off shopping, we enjoy ourselves making various pies for the festive season. It falls to me to be the teacher and for extra festive spirit (and in payment for my services!) everyone brings along a bottle of superb single-malt whisky. After we endure about 6 hours' work baking and sweating in a cottage kitchen – and the hardship of tasting the whiskies – our wives return and we present them with our festive feast.

When I first came to Scotland in the 1970s I was delighted by the variety and quality of the pies on offer. The choice of wonderful meats makes Scotland a truly ideal place for baking pies and pasties. I remember the intense, unique flavour of the small mutton pies, or tuppenny struggles, the venison pasties and Forfar bridies, and, being a pie fanatic, I was keen to taste an Ayrshire pork pie to compare it to the famous Melton Mowbray and other pork pies. There are too many different varieties for me to pin down my favourite but I must say that the Teviotdale pie – made with a suet pastry and the finest beef – is particularly delicious. Many of these pies can be bought ready-made but when you make your own, you can be sure that you've used the best ingredients.

making pastry – tips and advice

Here are a few tips and a little advice on pastry to make life that little bit easier.

- The equipment you use is very important in pastry-making. Always use a large bowl rather than a small bowl and a heavy rolling pin rather than a thin, light one.
- Keep all the ingredients, utensils and your hands as cool as possible.
- Roll in one direction only, not backwards and forwards, turning the pastry at right angles to obtain the required shape.
- Most chefs and professional bakers use plain flour when making puff pastry and savoury pies; it makes the pastry crisper than self-raising, which aerates during the baking process, making the pastry softer.
- Always sift plain flour to avoid lumps.
- If you are making shortcrust, allow the butter or fats to soften slightly before you start. This will ensure that it is not difficult to rub into the flour. However, when making puff pastry, the butter and fats must be chilled.
- When rolling out pastry, always use a lightly floured flat surface or pastry board. Shape the pastry first either into a circle or oblong. Lightly dust the rolling pin with flour and roll with both hands, keeping the pressure even. Give the pastry a quarter-turn and roll away from you, repeating this process until it is the size you require.
- I always roll the pastry out slightly larger than required and use the excess to make leaf shapes to decorate my pies.
- Heat is vital in the art of pastry-making so always preheat the oven and for a really crisp base, preheat the baking sheet at the same time. This will conduct the heat evenly under the pie dish or tin.
- Where eggs are required, use free range: they have the edge over any other eggs and give extra colour to glazes.
- And finally, when adding salt, remember you can put it in but you cannot take it out – do not over-season!

shortcrust pastry

Makes 450 g/1 lb

350 g/12 oz plain flour
pinch salt
50 g/2 oz lard
100 g/4 oz butter
approximately 5 tbsp cold water

Sift the flour with the salt. Rub in the lard and butter until the mixture looks like breadcrumbs.

Gradually add the water and mix to a firm dough.

Chill for 20 minutes. Allow the pastry to relax for 10 minutes after rolling out.

rich shortcrust pastry

Makes 450 g/1 lb

350 g/12 oz plain flour
pinch salt
200 g/7 oz butter
1 free-range egg yolk, beaten
approximately 5 tbsp cold water

Sift the flour with the salt. Rub in the butter until the mixture looks like breadcrumbs. Mix the yolk with the water and then add to the other ingredients.

Mix to a firm dough.

Chill for 20 minutes. Allow the pastry to relax for 10 minutes after rolling out.

wholemeal shortcrust pastry

Makes 450 g/1 lb

   110 g/4 oz wholemeal flour
   110 g/4 oz self-raising flour
   pinch salt
   50 g/2 oz butter
   50 g/2 oz lard
   approximately 3 tbsp cold water

Mix the flours with the salt. Rub in the butter and lard until the mixture looks like breadcrumbs.

Gradually add the water and mix to a firm dough.

Chill for 20 minutes. Allow the pastry to relax for 10 minutes after rolling out.

savoury pasty pastry

Makes 450 g/1 lb

   175 g/6 oz lard
   350 g/12 oz plain flour
   approximately 100 ml/3 fl. oz water
   salt
   freshly milled black pepper

Sift the flour. Add the salt and pepper. Rub in the lard until the mixture looks like breadcrumbs.

Gradually add the water and mix to a firm dough.

Place the pastry in a plastic bag and refrigerate for 20 minutes.

my mother and gran's suet crust pastry

My family made this pastry for steamed puddings but I recommend using it for an oven-baked game pie, too.

Makes 450 g/1 lb

350 g/12 oz self-raising flour
175 g/6 oz shredded beef suet
salt
freshly milled black pepper
approximately 100 ml/3 fl. oz cold water

Sift the flour into a bowl, then add the suet and seasoning, and mix in lightly with your hands. Add some cold water and mix it in with a sharp knife for the first minute and then with your fingers until all the ingredients are well combined and the sides of the bowl are clean.

Let the pastry rest for 10 minutes, then roll it out.

traditional suet crust

This recipe comes from Rosa Lewis, who was cook at the Cavendish Hotel, London, at the turn of the nineteenth century. She was a regular visitor to Scotland and always came back with plenty of game for her pies. Lewis was renowned for her suet crust, which she made for King Edward VII on many occasions.

Makes 450 g/1 lb

220 g/8 oz self-raising flour
1 level tsp baking powder
salt
freshly ground white pepper
pinch mace
pinch ground rosemary
110 g/4 oz beef suet
approximately 60 ml/2 fl. oz cold water

Sift the flour, baking powder, salt, pepper and spices. Lightly toss in the beef suet and stir in loosely with a fork. Make a well in the centre of the mixture and add just enough water to make a workable dough. Knead for a few minutes only. The suet crust is ready for use immediately.

quick flaky pastry

Makes 450 g/1 lb

225 g/8 oz plain flour
175 g/6 oz butter
approximately 60 ml/2 fl. oz cold water

Sift the flour into a bowl, then rub in the butter and blend thoroughly until the mixture looks like breadcrumbs.

Gradually add the water and mix to a firm dough.

Place the pastry in a plastic bag and refrigerate for 30 minutes.

hot-water pastry

Makes 450 g/1 lb

150 g/5 oz lard
200 ml/7 fl. oz hot water
350 g/12 oz plain flour, seasoned with ½ tsp salt
1 large free-range egg yolk

Put the lard and water into a saucepan and heat gently until the lard has melted. Bring to the boil, remove from the heat and beat in the seasoned flour to form a soft dough. Beat the egg yolk into the dough, cover with a damp cloth and rest in a warm place for 15 minutes. Do not allow the pastry to cool before rolling out.

rough puff pastry

Makes 1.25 kg/3 lb

450 g/1 lb strong plain flour
pinch salt
approximately 350 ml/12 fl. oz cold water
juice of half a lemon
450 g/1 lb unsalted butter, chilled

Sift the flour and salt into a bowl and mix to a firm dough with the water and lemon juice. Wrap in greaseproof paper and rest in the fridge for 25 minutes.

Roll the dough into a square about 1 cm/½ in. thick. Cut the butter into 2 cm/1-in. dice and scatter into the centre of the square. Fold the dough over the edges of the butter to make a parcel.

Flour your work surface and flatten the dough with a rolling pin. Roll out into a rectangle approximately 45 cm/18 in. x 15 cm/6 in. Fold the outer thirds of the rectangle into the centre, aligning the sides and sealing the edges.

Turn the dough 90 degrees. Repeat the folding process, again sealing the edges. Cover with clingfilm and refrigerate for a further 30 minutes.

Repeat the process, flouring the work surface and flattening the dough with a rolling pin, rolling it out into a rectangle and folding the edges into the centre, the edges aligned and sealed.

Turn the dough 90 degrees and repeat the folding process. Cover with clingfilm and refrigerate for a further 30 minutes, after which the pastry will be ready for use.

traditional puff pastry

Makes 450 g/1 lb

  225 g/8 oz plain flour
  pinch salt
  30 g/1 oz lard
  150 ml/⅓ pt ice-cold water
  2 tbsp lemon juice
  200 g/7 oz butter, chilled

Sift the flour with the salt. Gently rub in the lard with your fingers. Add the cold water and lemon juice and mix with a knife to a dough. Turn the dough onto the table or worktop and knead very quickly until it is smooth. Wrap in clingfilm and leave in the fridge for 30 minutes.

Roll the dough into a square about 1 cm/½ in. thick. Cut the butter into 2 cm/1 in. dice and scatter into the centre of the square. Fold the dough over the edges of the butter to make a parcel.

Flour your work surface and flatten the dough with a rolling pin. Roll out into a rectangle approximately 45 cm/18 in. x 15 cm/6 in. Fold the outer thirds of the rectangle into the centre, aligning the sides and sealing the edges.

Turn the dough 90 degrees. Repeat the folding process, again sealing the edges. Cover with clingfilm and refrigerate for a further 30 minutes.

Repeat the process, flouring the work surface and flattening the dough with a rolling pin, rolling it out into a rectangle and folding the edges into the centre, the edges aligned and sealed.

Turn the dough 90 degrees and repeat the folding process. Cover with clingfilm and refrigerate for a further 30 minutes, after which the pastry will be ready for use.

a standing crust for great pies

Take a Peck of Flour, and six Pounds of Butter, boiled in a Gallon of Water, skim it off into the Flour, and as little of the Liquor as you can; work it well into a paste, then pull it into Pieces till it is cold, then make it up in what Form you will have it. This is fit for the Walls of a Goose pye.

The Art of Cookery Made Plain and Easy, Mrs Hannah Glasse (1747)

tuppenny struggles

These small mutton pies were part of the culture of Scotland in the early nineteenth century, when the pieman toured the streets, the sound of his bell competing with the clanging voices of the oyster-women as they sold their wares.

You can use mutton but I recommend lamb, as it is now much cheaper. You will need 6 small pie tins.

Makes 6

450 g/1 lb hot-water pastry (see p. 142)
450 g/1 lb lean lamb, minced
salt
freshly milled black pepper
pinch freshly grated nutmeg
275 ml/½ pt lamb stock
1 free-range egg, beaten with a little milk

Preheat the oven to 200°C/400°F/Gas Mark 6.

Prepare the hot-water pastry and set one-third aside in a warm area for the pie lids. Line the 6 small tins (about 10 cm/4 in. in diameter) with greaseproof paper. Roll out the pastry and line the tins, patting the pastry into the base and sides and making sure it is evenly distributed.

In a large bowl, season the mince well with salt, pepper and nutmeg. Add just enough stock to moisten the meat. Divide the meat equally between the pie tins.

Cover the tops with the remaining pastry and make a small hole in the centre of each lid. Glaze the pies with the beaten egg and place them on a baking tray.

Bake in the centre of the oven for 1 hour, lowering the heat after 10 minutes to 180°C/350°F/Gas Mark 4.

ayrshire pork pie

This is based on a 200-year-old recipe and is as near to the original as a modern-day cook will get.

The received wisdom is that the Ayrshire pork pie, like the Melton Mowbray, became popular because it was a 'hunting pie' – a convenient picnic food. But I am convinced that it gained its classic status because the flavours in the filling are so different from those of ordinary pork pies.

Serves 4–6

700 g/1½ lb hot-water pastry (see p. 142)
900 g/2 lb Ayrshire pork shoulder
   (⅓ fat), skin and gristle removed,
   in very small dice, about 5 mm/¼ in.
1 tsp anchovy essence
generous pinch salt
generous pinch white pepper
1 free-range egg, beaten

FOR THE PORK STOCK:
900 g/2 lb pork bones
1 pig's foot
600 ml/1 pt water
1 large onion, peeled
1 carrot
1 bay leaf
2 sage leaves
sprig thyme
sprig marjoram
salt
6 peppercorns

First, make the stock: put all the ingredients in a large pan and bring to the boil. Reduce the heat and simmer for 2 hours or more until the stock has reduced to 300 ml/½ pt.

Check the seasoning, let it cool and skim off all the fat. Strain the stock through a fine non-metallic sieve and place to one side.

Combine the pork shoulder, anchovy essence, salt and pepper in a bowl with 2 tablespoons of the pork stock.

Preheat the oven to 180°C/350°F/Gas Mark 4.

Make up the hot-water pastry.

Roll out the pastry and pat two-thirds of it into a lightly greased pie mould or cake tin about 18 cm/7 in. in diameter with hinged sides and a detachable base. Make sure the pastry is evenly distributed. Reserve the rest for the top of the pie.

Place the tin on a baking tray and put in the seasoned pork filling. Roll out the rest of the pastry and top the pie with it, firmly crimping the edges and being very careful not to tear the pastry. Make a hole in the centre of the lid to allow the steam out during the cooking process. Bake in the lower part of the oven for 2 hours.

Ten minutes before the cooking time is up, glaze the pie with the beaten egg and return it to the oven.

Turn the oven off without opening the door and leave the pie in the oven for 1 hour to dry naturally.

Reheat the stock until just warm and pour as much as the pie will hold into the hole in the centre of the lid.

Let the pie cool, wrap it in clingfilm and refrigerate for at least a day. Take one slice from the pie and hide before letting the family devour your hard work.

a ham pye

I adore this recipe. It is so detailed and has so much to tell us about how flexible and resourceful cooks were at that time – wonderfully informative.

Slice some cold boiled ham about half an inch thick, make a good crust, and thick, over the dish, and lay a layer of ham, shake a little pepper over it, then take a large young fowl clean plucked, gutted, washed and singed; put a little pepper and salt in the belly, and rub a very little salt on the outside; lay the fowl on the ham, boil some eggs hard, put in the yolks, and cover all with ham, then shake some pepper on the ham, and put on a top crust. Bake it well, have ready when it comes out of the oven some very rich beef-gravy, enough to fill the pye, lay on the crust again, and send it to the table hot. A fresh ham will not be so tender; so that I always boil my ham one day, and bring it to the table, and make a pye of it. It does better than an unboiled ham. If you put two large fowls in they will make a fine pye. But that is according to your company, more or less. The crust must be the same you make for venison pasty. You should pour a little strong gravy into the pye when you bake it, just to bake the meat, and then fill it up when it comes out of the oven. Boil some truffles and morels, and put into the pye, it is a great addition; and fresh mushrooms or dried ones.

Taken from *The Whole Art of Cookery Made Easy and Familiar by William Gelleroy, Late Cook to Her Grace the Duchess of Argyle* (1762)

beef wellington

Or is it Brontë's pie? Writing to her sister Emily on 1 December 1843, Charlotte wished she could be in the kitchen at Haworth Parsonage cutting up a meat hash and topping it with pastry to be baked in the oven.

You can make this Wellington in individual portions by dividing the recipe ingredients up in four after cooking the onions and mushrooms. For a truly Scottish version, top with haggis instead of chicken liver pâté.

Serves 4

450 g/1 lb puff pastry (bought or see p. 144)
900 g/2 lb fillet of Scottish beef
salt
freshly milled black pepper
75 g/3 oz butter
1 large red onion, finely chopped
175 g/6 oz wild mushrooms
175 g/6 oz chicken liver pâté or haggis
1 free-range egg, lightly beaten

Make up the puff pastry.

Preheat the oven to 200°C/400°F/Gas Mark 6.

With a sharp knife, carefully trim the fat from the beef fillet. Season the meat well with salt and pepper. Melt the butter in a large frying pan and add the beef, sealing it all over, cooking for at least 6 minutes. Remove the fillet from the pan and place it to one side to cool.

Add a little more butter to the same pan and add the chopped onion and mushrooms, cooking until all the moisture has evaporated. Season well and allow to cool.

Put a little of the pastry aside to use for decoration. Roll out the rest into a large rectangle and place on a lightly greased baking tray.

Completely coat the pastry with the onion and mushroom mixture and place the fillet of beef on top. Spread the pâté or haggis over the meat.

Brush the edges of the pastry with the beaten egg, then fold the pastry over, pressing the edges to seal it.

Make some flowers and leaves from the reserved pastry and brush all over with the beaten egg.

Bake in the centre of the oven for 20 minutes and then lower the temperature to 180°C/350°F/Gas Mark 4 and bake for a further 15 minutes until the pastry is golden brown.

Let the Wellington rest for at least 5 minutes before serving.

a famous grouse within grouse pie

In Scotland, grouse pie is traditionally served with fried bread and rowan jelly. True to form, I have combined these ingredients in this truly traditional grouse pie, using Famous Grouse whisky for flavour.

Serves 4–6

275 g/10 oz puff pastry (bought or see p. 144)
25 g/1 oz butter
1 tbsp cooking oil
450 ml/1 lb grouse meat
salt
freshly milled black pepper
6 slices rindless streaky bacon, finely chopped
8 shallots, peeled and sliced

1 small carrot, diced
85 ml/3 fl. oz Famous Grouse whisky
150 ml/¼ pt chicken stock (see p. 15)
2 tbsp double cream
5 tbsp rowan jelly
2 tbsp chopped fresh parsley
2 tbsp milk
2 slices white bread, cut into quarters
25 g/1 oz beef dripping
25 g/1 oz butter

Make up the pastry.

Preheat the oven to 200°C/400°F/Gas Mark 6.

Melt the butter with the cooking oil in a large saucepan. Add the grouse meat and seal all over, season with salt and pepper, and simmer for 3 minutes. Add the bacon, shallots and carrot, stirring briskly for a further 3 minutes. Add the whisky and chicken stock, bring to the boil and simmer for 25 minutes on a low heat, reducing the stock by at least one-third. Allow the grouse and sauce to cool slightly and blend in the double cream and rowan jelly.

Roll out the pastry to make a lid for a 1.1-litre/2-pint pie dish.

Place the mixture in the pie dish, sprinkle with freshly chopped parsley and cover with the puff-pastry lid. Wash the top with the milk and bake in the centre of the oven for 25 minutes.

Fry the bread in the dripping and butter, and arrange around the pie when it is ready to be served.

THE FAMOUS GROUSE MALT. MAKE AN ENTRANCE.

traditional game pie

Game pie is usually made with a puff pastry but I suggest giving this pie a suet crust.
Serves 6–8

50 g/2 oz butter
50 g/2 oz dripping or lard
775 g/1½ lb mixed game meat consisting of
    haunch of venison, rabbit and pheasant –
    pure meat, no gristle, all fat removed
225 g/8 oz button mushrooms
225 g/8 oz shallots, peeled
2 cloves garlic
3 tbsp seasoned plain flour
300 ml/½ pt claret
300 ml/½ pt beef stock (see p. 14)
1 onion, chopped
8 juniper berries
pinch allspice
pinch marjoram
1 tsp salt
freshly milled black pepper
700 g/1½ lb Gran's suet crust pastry (see p. 141)
2 tbsp milk

Preheat the oven to 180°C/350°F/Gas Mark 4.

In a very large saucepan, heat the fat gently, add the game meat and seal, cooking for 5 minutes, extracting the juices and browning the meat quickly.

Add the mushroom, shallots and garlic, cooking for a further 4 minutes. Sprinkle with the flour and cook for 3 minutes. Slowly add the wine and beef stock. Add the onion, juniper berries, allspice and marjoram, season, take the pan from the heat and allow to stand for 6 hours.

Meanwhile, make up the pastry, leaving it covered in a warm place until required.

Bring the game mix to the boil and simmer, reducing the stock by half, cooking for at least 25 minutes.

Place the filling in a 1.1-litre/2-pint pie dish.

Roll out the pastry and cover the pie dish, sealing all round. Brush with a little milk and bake in the centre of the oven for 50 minutes.

kitchiner's pigeon or lark pie

This recipe is taken from Dr William Kitchiner's 1817 book *The Cook's Oracle*. My biography, *Dr William Kitchiner: Regency Eccentric*, was shortlisted for the André Simon Award in 1993, and my co-author Colin Cooper English and I are proud to say we came second.

Truss half a dozen fine large Pigeons as for stewing, season them with Pepper and Salt: lay at the bottom of the dish a Rump Steak of about a pound weight, cut into pieces and trimmed neatly, seasoned and beat out with a chopper: on it lay the pigeons, the yolks of three Eggs boiled hard, and a gill of broth or water, and over these a layer of steaks. Wet the edge of the dish, and cover it over with Puff-paste, or the paste as directed for seasoned pies. Wash it over with Yolk of Egg, and ornament it with leaves of paste, and the feet of the Pigeons; bake it an hour and a half in a moderate heated oven: before it is sent to table make an aperture in the top, and pour in some good Gravy quite hot.

The bird's feet were often added to show what was in the pie. Another recipe of the period suggests that the feet should be left poking through a hole in the pastry.

For a modernised version of this dish, see pheasant and beefsteak pie on p. 165 and replace the pheasant with pigeon.

partan pie

This is one of the most unusual pie recipes you will ever see or taste, from the windy coast of Fife. Making a crab pie would have been a very messy job 10 years ago; it is not any more, because you can buy crab meat anywhere, without the hassle of extracting it from the shell yourself with skewers and nutcrackers.

I like to cook the crab mixture in oyster shells. Traditionally, this would be served with oatmeal cobs and lashings of fresh butter.

Makes 4 small pies

450 g/1 lb crab meat, brown and white
salt
freshly ground white pepper
½ tsp freshly grated nutmeg
3 tbsp white wine vinegar
2 tbsp Arran mustard
75 g/3 oz soft brown breadcrumbs
30 g/1 oz butter

Preheat the oven to 180°C/350°F/Gas Mark 4.

Season the crab meat well with the salt, pepper and freshly grated nutmeg and blend the ingredients thoroughly.

Place the mixture into shells or ovenproof ramekins.

Gently heat the vinegar and mustard together and pour over the crab meat.

Cover the crab meat with a layer of breadcrumbs and dot the top of the breadcrumbs with butter. Place in the centre of the oven for 15 minutes.

flaky wild salmon pie

Fish pie is a traditional dish throughout Britain. In Scotland they use fresh salmon or finnan haddock, in Cornwall, haddock with some white crab meat, while Northern folk are cod-lovers.

You can add some prawns to this pie if you wish or top with mashed potato instead of pastry.

Serves 4

450 g/1 lb fresh wild salmon, boned and skinned
600 ml/1 pt milk
25 g/1 oz butter
25 g/1 oz flour
1 tsp capers
1 tbsp lemon juice
2 tbsp chopped fresh parsley
salt
freshly milled black pepper
350 g/12 oz quick flaky pastry (see p. 142)
1 free-range egg, beaten

Place the salmon in a large saucepan and cover with milk. Simmer for about 10 minutes. Strain the milk into a bowl and place the salmon to one side.

Melt the butter in the saucepan and then add the flour, cook for 3 minutes and then slowly return the milk back to the saucepan, stirring all the time until the sauce thickens. Add the capers, lemon juice and parsley, season and stir. Break the salmon into flakes with a fork and mix it into the sauce. Allow the mixture to cool.

Make up the pastry.

Preheat the oven to 220°C/425°F/Gas Mark 8.

Put the salmon filling into a pie dish and top with the pastry. Crimp the edges and glaze with the beaten egg. Bake in the centre of the oven for 30 minutes.

Serve with new potatoes and mint peas.

slow-cooked aberdeen angus steak in whisky sauce with a puff-pastry topping

When meat is cooked slowly like this, the flavours develop more intensity, so it is essential you use a good-quality whisky, whether blended or single malt.

Serves 4–6

I tbsp cooking oil
750 g/1¾ lb Aberdeen Angus braising steak, trimmed of any fat and cubed
300 g/10 oz shallots, peeled
250 g/9 oz carrots, diced
250 g/9 oz parsnip, diced
330 ml/11 fl. oz stout
150 ml/⅓ pt whisky
450 ml/¾ pt beef stock (see p. 14)
250 g/9 oz button mushrooms, sliced
2 bay leaves
450 g/1 lb puff pastry (bought or see p. 144)
2 tbsp redcurrant jelly
I tsp wholegrain mustard
I tbsp cornflour, blended with a little cold water
I tbsp chopped fresh thyme
salt
freshly milled black pepper
I free-range egg, beaten with a little milk

Heat the cooking oil in a large flameproof casserole dish, add half the steak and cook quickly until browned on all sides, then remove from the pan. Add the remaining meat and brown in the same way.

Return all the meat to the pan with the shallots, carrots and parsnips. Add the stout, whisky, stock, mushrooms and bay leaves. Bring to the boil, then cover and simmer gently for 1 hour, until the meat is tender.

Meanwhile, make up the pastry.

Preheat the oven to 180°C/350°F/Gas Mark 4.

Mix the redcurrant jelly and mustard into the steak mixture. Stir in the cornflour and thyme, and season to taste before topping with puff pastry. Brush the pastry with the beaten egg and place the dish in the oven for a final 30 minutes.

forfar bridies

Invented by Mr Jolly, a baker in Forfar, around the 1870s. Why bridies? Because they are a simple meal that a young bride could easily add to her repertoire.

Serve with a glass of Veryberry wine from the Orkney Wine Company – delicious.
Makes 4–6

450 g/1 lb shortcrust pastry (see p. 139)
450 g /1 lb rump steak, diced
75 g/3 oz beef suet
2 onions, finely chopped
1 tbsp chopped fresh parsley
salt
freshly milled black pepper
1 free-range egg, beaten with a little milk

Make up the pastry.

Preheat the oven to 200°C/400°F/Gas Mark 6.

Roll out the pastry to about 5 mm/¼ in. thick and cut out 4–6 rounds of about 15 cm/6 in.

Place the steak, suet, chopped onions and parsley in a bowl and season well, mixing all the ingredients together. Put an equal amount of the mixture in the centre of each round.

Dampen the edge of the pastry with the beaten egg and fold over to make a half-moon shape. Turn the edges round to make small 'turns' (horns), pinching and crimping the edges to seal completely. Glaze the bridies with the beaten egg and place on a greased baking tray.

Bake in the centre of the oven for 45 minutes, lowering the heat after 10 minutes to 180°C/350°F/Gas Mark 4.

teviotdale pie

While I was writing this section, I had a visit from a friend of mine, Ted Weaver. I took him into my kitchen where I had the finished pie ready for a photograph. After the photo shoot, Ted made the pie disappear in minutes. This really is every pie-lover's favourite and a most popular pie around Britain at the moment, not only in the home kitchen but also in restaurants, cafes and hotels.

The pie comes from the Scottish Borders and was originally made with minced beef and some added vegetables but it is the suet that makes it taste so good. Use the best Aberdeen Angus rump steak and ox kidney to achieve the perfect pie – please do not substitute cheap cuts of meat. Should you want to make a steak and ale version, then omit the kidney and soak the steak in 150 ml/¼ pt beer overnight and add the beer marinade to the stock.

Serves 6

575 g/1¼ lb rump steak
175 g/6 oz ox kidney
1 large red onion, chopped
25 g/1 oz seasoned flour
25 g/1 oz butter
300 ml/½ pt beef stock (see p. 14)
salt
freshly milled black pepper

FOR THE SUET BATTER:
225 g/8 oz self-raising flour
75 g/3 oz fresh beef suet
30 g/1 oz cornflour
300 ml/½ pt fresh milk
salt
freshly milled black pepper

Preheat the oven to 180°C/350°F/Gas Mark 4.

Trim the steak of any skin and fat and cut into 2.5-cm/1-in. cubes. Remove the fat, skin and core from the kidney and dice it quite small. Toss the steak and kidney in the seasoned flour.

In a large frying pan, melt the butter and quickly seal the meat all over. Add the chopped onion and cook for 4 minutes.

Add the beef stock, season and simmer for an hour.

While the beef is cooking, make up the suet batter: put the self-raising flour, suet and cornflour into a large bowl, season well and slowly add the milk, whisking, until the mixture has the consistency of a thick batter.

Put the steak filling into a 1.1-litre/2-pint pudding basin or pie dish and cover with the suet batter mixture. Bake in the centre of the oven for 35 to 40 minutes.

chicken and mushroom pasty

The pasty was eaten by coal miners in Scotland as a more convenient and practical version of the sandwich – the pastry protected the filling from the dust and dirt of the mine. The miners, when they could not afford chicken, often used sausage meat.

Makes 6–8

50 g/2 oz butter
450 g/1 lb chicken breast, roughly chopped
100 g/4 oz small button mushrooms, cleaned and finely chopped
2 sprigs fresh parsley, chopped
3 tbsp redcurrant jelly
225 g/8 oz potatoes, cooked and diced
salt
freshly milled black pepper
450 g/1 lb savoury pasty pastry (see p. 140)
1 free-range egg, beaten with a little milk

Preheat the oven to 180°C/350°F/Gas Mark 4.

Melt the butter in a frying pan, add the chicken meat, mushrooms and parsley, cover and cook for 20 minutes, stirring every 5 minutes. Add the jelly and potatoes, season well and allow to cool.

Meanwhile, make up the pastry, roll it out until it is 5 mm/¼ in. thick and cut out 8 rounds of 15 cm/6 in.

Place some chicken mixture in the centre of each round, dampen the edges of the pastry with a little of the beaten egg and fold over to make a half-moon shape, pinching and crimping the edges.

Glaze the pasties all over with the beaten egg and put them on a greased baking tray. Bake for 35 minutes.

Serve with a crisp vegetable salad.

christmas poacher's pie

Game is always popular at Christmas, especially in Scotland, home of the poacher's pie. The winter months were the height of the game season and poachers would go out hunting for a special festive pie.

For extra flavour, line the base of the pie dish with 150 g/5 oz of haggis.

Serves 8

450 g/1 lb rough puff pastry (see p. 143)
225 g/8 oz boned rabbit, skinned and cubed
225 g/8 oz boned grouse, skinned and cubed
225 g/8 oz boned pheasant, skinned and cubed
salt
freshly milled black pepper
100 g/4 oz rindless streaky bacon, chopped
1 large leek, washed and sliced
2 potatoes, sliced
1 tbsp chopped fresh parsley
pinch thyme
150 ml/⅓ pt chicken stock (see p. 15)

Preheat the oven to 190°C/375°F/Gas Mark 5.

Make up the pastry.

Mix the game meats together, season well. Fill a large pie dish with a layer of game, followed by a layer of bacon and vegetables and so on. Add the herbs and just enough chicken stock to half-fill the pie dish.

Roll out the pastry on a lightly floured surface until it is the right size to cover the pie dish.

Trim and seal the edges, making a small hole in the centre of the pastry lid to let out the steam. Brush the top with the beaten egg.

Cover loosely with greased kitchen foil and bake in the oven for 1 hour 35 minutes, reducing the heat to 180°C/350°F/Gas Mark 4 after 35 minutes.

rabbit pie

Rabbit is more popular today than it has ever been. You can find rabbit at most Farmers' Markets across the UK and may I suggest that you visit them regularly – they are the best places to shop for freshness and it's great fun seeing the different varieties of produce on offer.

Serves 6-8

25 g/1 oz beef dripping
675 g/1½ lb roughly chopped rabbit meat
450 g/1 lb potatoes, peeled and diced
150 g/5 oz diced carrot
2 large onions, peeled and sliced
1 tbsp mixed herbs
25 g/1 oz plain flour
300 ml/10 fl. oz game or chicken stock (see p. 15)
salt
freshly milled black pepper
225 g/8 oz black pudding, skin removed, diced
450 g/1 lb Gran's suet crust pastry (see p. 141)
1 free-range egg, beaten with a little milk

In a large saucepan, warm the dripping until it is quite hot, add the rabbit and very quickly seal and brown, cooking for 5 minutes.

Add the potatoes, carrot, onion and mixed herbs, cooking for 4 minutes. Sprinkle with the flour, stir, add the stock and bring to the boil. Reduce the heat and simmer for 40 minutes.

Meanwhile, make up the pastry.

Preheat the oven to 200°C/400°F/Gas Mark 6.

Season the rabbit mixture with salt and pepper, and put it into a 1.1-litre/2-pint pie dish, scattering the diced black pudding over the top (this helps to thicken the pie during the cooking process).

Roll out the pastry to cover the pie dish, sealing and crimping all around. Trim off any excess pastry and use to make leaves for decoration. Brush with the egg wash and bake in the centre of the oven for 30–45 minutes, until the pastry is golden brown and crisp.

MEG DODS' VENISON PASTY

This recipe comes from the best-known Scottish cookbook of its day, *The Cook and Housewife's Manual.* Written by Christina Jane Johnstone, it was published in 1826 under the nom de plume Meg Dods, the name of the landlady in Sir Walter Scott's *St Ronan's Well.* Here is her original recipe, followed by my modernised version. You will notice that the dish is not what you might expect — when we think of a pasty, we think of a half-moon-shaped pastry filled with meat but this is something altogether grander.

A modern pasty is made of what does not roast well, as the neck, the breast, the shoulder. The breast makes a good pasty. Cut into little chops, trimming off all bones and skins. Make some good gravy from the bones and other trimmings. Place fat and lean pieces of meat together, or, if very lean, place thin slices from the firm fat of a leg or a neck of mutton along with each piece.

Season the meat with pepper, salt, pounded mace, and allspice. Place it handsomely in a dish and put in the drawn gravy, a quarter-pint of claret or port, a glassful of eschalot vinegar, and, if liked, a couple of onions very finely shred. Cover the dish with a thick crust.

venison pasty

Serves 4–6

675 g/1½ lb loin of venison
50 g/2 oz butter
1 tbsp cooking oil
1 red onion, finely chopped
2 tbsp flour
290 ml/½ pt game stock (see p. 16)
½ tsp mace
½ tsp allspice
150 ml/⅓ pt of claret
2 tbsp shallot vinegar
2 tbsp rowan jelly
freshly milled black pepper
salt
450 g/1 lb hot-water pastry (see p. 142)
1 free-range egg, beaten with a little milk

Cut the venison into 5 cm/2 in. cubes, trimming away any tough membrane or sinew. Heat the butter and oil in a large saucepan, add the venison and onion, and brown the meat, cooking for about 4 minutes.

Add the flour and cook for a further 3 minutes, then pour in the game stock and cook for 10 minutes. Slowly add the spices, wine, vinegar and jelly, season, blend thoroughly and simmer for 30 minutes.

Preheat the oven to 180°C/350°F/Gas Mark 4.

Make up the pastry and roll it out while it is still warm. Reserve some of the pastry and use it to make leaves to decorate the top of the pie.

Allow the venison filling to cool slightly and then place into a deep pie dish. Top with the pastry, decorating with the pastry leaves arranged in a circle. Wash with the beaten egg and place in the oven for 80 minutes. Allow the pasty to rest for 5 minutes before serving with some minted new potatoes and boiled fresh beetroot.

luxury fish pie
with oatmeal potato topping

When I was reading Pamela Stephenson's fascinating and entertaining biography of her husband Billy Connolly, aptly entitled *Billy*, I found out that he cooked a fish pie followed by clootie dumpling for Christmas dinner during their stay in LA. I was inspired to create this recipe, which would make an excellent Connolly family dinner.

Serves 4

250 g/8 oz salmon fillet, skinned
250 g/8 oz cod fillet, skinned
250 g/8 oz naturally cured finnan haddock
100 g/4 oz spring onions, finely chopped
1 tbsp lemon juice
100 g/4 oz button mushrooms, sliced
1 bay leaf
300 ml/½ pt milk
pinch saffron
pinch nutmeg
25 g/1 oz unsalted butter

25 g/1 oz seasoned flour
FOR THE MASH TOPPING:
450 g/1 lb mashed potato
25 g/1 oz butter
25 g/1 oz oatmeal
2 tbsp double cream
100 g/4 oz Scottish cheddar cheese, grated (optional)

Preheat the oven to 190°C/375°F/Gas Mark 5.

Place the fish, spring onions, lemon juice, mushrooms and bay leaf in a saucepan. Pour over the milk and slowly bring to the boil. Add the saffron and nutmeg, cover and simmer for 10 minutes. Carefully remove the fish and vegetables. Strain the liquid into a bowl and reserve. Discard any fish bones and the bay leaf.

Melt the butter in a saucepan, gradually adding the flour, and cook gently for 2 minutes. Slowly add the reserved milk. Bring to the boil and simmer for 2 minutes, until the sauce thickens and becomes very smooth. Add the fish and vegetables.

Place the mixture in a deep 2-litre ovenproof serving dish and allow to cool.

Blend together the mashed potato, butter, oatmeal and cream and use this mixture to cover completely the fish filling. Sprinkle all over with the grated cheese, if wished, and bake in the centre of the oven for 30 minutes until golden brown.

Serve with mange tout and roasted parsnips.

pheasant and beefsteak pie

In the eighteenth and nineteenth centuries, oysters were very cheap and would often be added to this pie to help eke out the other ingredients. The unusual combination became a classic and can still be found in traditional hotels and game restaurants. Should you wish to be bold, add a dozen fresh or smoked oysters just before you cover the pie with pastry.

Serves 6

25 g/1 oz beef dripping
340 g/12 oz pheasant meat, cut into chunks
450 g/1 lb rump steak, cut into chunks
225 g/½ lb button mushrooms
1 bay leaf
sprig thyme
1 tsp chopped fresh parsley
10 shallots, peeled and sliced
salt
freshly milled black pepper
1 tbsp plain flour
190 ml/7 fl. oz beef stock (see p. 14)
150 ml/⅓ pt red wine
285 g/10 oz puff pastry (bought or see p. 144)
1 free-range egg, beaten with a little milk

Heat the dripping in a large saucepan and brown the meat all over, cooking for about 4 minutes. Add the mushrooms, bay leaf, thyme, parsley and shallots, and cook for a further 3 minutes, seasoning with salt and pepper. Sprinkle over the flour and cook for 3 minutes. Add the beef stock and red wine, and simmer gently for 1 hour.

Meanwhile, make up the pastry.

Carefully discard the bay leaf and thyme from the meat mixture. With a slotted spoon, remove the meat and mushrooms from the saucepan and place in a deep pie dish.

Preheat the oven to 180°C/350°F/Gas Mark 4.

Reduce the liquid in the saucepan by half.

Roll out the puff pastry to fit the pie dish.

Pour the liquid onto the meat and top with the pastry. Generously wash the top of the pastry with the beaten egg and bake in the centre of the oven for 40 minutes.

aberdeen angus beefsteak pudding

What to serve with this beefsteak pudding? What would the readers of this book enjoy? I feel a rustic bubble and squeak such as that on p. 48 and some roast parsnips would be perfect.

Serves 4

700 g/1½ lb traditional suet crust pastry (see p. 141)
25 g/1 oz beef dripping
675 g/1½ lb Aberdeen Angus rump steak, fat removed, cut into chunks
2 large red onions, finely chopped
40 g/1½ oz plain flour
freshly grated nutmeg
425 ml/14 fl. oz beef stock (see p. 14)
50 ml/2 fl. oz port
salt
freshly milled black pepper
1 tbsp chopped fresh parsley

Make up the pastry and roll it out. Butter a 1.35 kg/3 lb pudding basin and line with the pastry, reserving enough to make the lid.

In a large saucepan, heat the dripping and fry the steak for 4 minutes. Add the onion and cook for a further 2 minutes. Sprinkle with the flour and grate over a little nutmeg, cooking for 3 more minutes. Add the beef stock, port, seasoning and parsley, and simmer for 20 minutes. Remove from the heat and allow to cool.

Place the filling into the suet-lined pudding basin.

Roll out the remaining suet to make the lid and cover the pudding, dampening the edges with a little water and pressing down to seal.

Cover the pudding with a doubled-up piece of greaseproof paper and secure it with string, leaving room for the pastry to expand.

Half-fill a large saucepan with a tight-fitting lid with water and bring to the boil. Place the pudding basin carefully in the saucepan of boiling water, cover and steam for 2 hours, taking great care to top up with boiling water.

Leave to stand for 10 minutes before serving. Pour any juices that remain in the basin into a sauceboat and serve with the pudding.

sweet puddings and desserts

Some Scottish delicacies in this section include the famous clootie dumpling, my all-time favourite, Drambuie tart, an unusual, traditional rice pie, a heart-warming marmalade roly-poly and a chocolate pudding that you will want to make again and again. Chef Jeff Bland gives us his spectacular version of strawberry shortcake, which he serves at the Balmoral Hotel in Edinburgh, and there's a recipe for cranachan, which is simple to make and a wonderfully refreshing way to round off a meal.

cranachan

This really is a classic. Also known as cream crowdie, cranachan is often served on Burns Night along with the clootie dumpling.

You can add a dram of whisky with the oatmeal and honey but children love this recipe so I have omitted it here.

For Shona – thank you.

Serves 4

75 ml/3 oz oatmeal
600 ml/1 pt double cream
3 tbsp heather honey
250 g/9 oz raspberries

Place the oatmeal on a tray and toast it for a few minutes under a hot grill.

Whip the cream until thick and add the oatmeal and honey, blending the mixture thoroughly. Reserve 25g/1 oz of the raspberries and divide the rest between individual dishes. Pour over the cream mixture, top with the remaining rapberries and chill until required.

butterscotch tart

This recipe really is special. Butterscotch originated around the year 1666, when a Scots merchant brought his cargo of West Indian sugar to the Clyde and Scotland, providing Scotland with a unique dessert. The Scottish sweet tooth was a factor in the establishment of the great sugar-refining industry at Greenock.

Serves 4–6

175 g/6 oz rich shortcrust pastry (see p. 139)
50 g/2 oz sifted plain flour
175 g/6 oz demerara sugar
5 tbsp water
150 ml/⅓ pt buttermilk
50 g/2 oz butter
1 free-range egg yolk
pinch ground ginger
2 tbsp double cream
25 g/1 oz chopped walnuts

Preheat the oven to 190°C/375°F/Gas Mark 5.

Roll out the pastry and line a 20 cm/8 in. flan ring with it. Bake blind: line the raw pastry case with a double sheet of greaseproof paper or cooking foil and fill it with dried peas, beans or rice. This prevents the pastry bubbling during the cooking process. After 15 minutes, the dried peas and the greaseproof paper can be removed. Return the pastry case to the oven for a further 5 minutes. You can use the dried peas, beans or rice for the same purpose over and over again.

Gently heat the flour and sugar in a saucepan, blending them together and adding the water. Boil the buttermilk in another saucepan and pour it over the flour and sugar, mixing them thoroughly. Cut the butter into small pieces and slowly add to the pan, stirring all the time.

Remove the pan from the heat, blend in the egg yolk, ginger and cream, allow to settle for 30 seconds and then mix again. Pour the butterscotch filling into the baked pastry case and top with the chopped walnuts.

Refrigerate for at least 1 hour.

old-fashioned 18 carat trifle

A good summer treat when you want to taste something completely different. I experimented with this golden, spicy wine from the Orkney Wine Company (see Recommended Suppliers) and I declare the result to be an 18 carat success! However, if you wish, a good malt whisky could be used as a substitute.

Serves 4

FOR THE SPONGE FINGERS:
100 g/4 oz plain flour
3 free-range eggs, separated
100 g/4 oz castor sugar

4 tbsp raspberry jam
6 tbsp 18 Carat wine
25 g/1 oz flaked almonds
zest of ½ lemon, grated
500 ml/17 fl. oz custard sauce (see p. 173)
300 ml/½ pt double cream
25 g/1 oz crushed almonds
glacé cherries

First make the sponge fingers.

Preheat the oven to 160°C/325°F/Gas Mark 3.

Butter two 25 cm x 10 in. baking trays. Dust the trays lightly with castor sugar.

Sift the flour into a bowl.

Blend together the egg yolks and sugar in a clean bowl and lightly fold in half the flour.

Whisk the egg whites until they become firm, fold them very lightly into the yolk mixture and add the remaining flour.

Spoon the mixture into thin fingers on the baking trays, spacing them well to allow them to spread. Bake in the centre of the oven for 12 minutes. Allow to cool completely.

Coat the sponge fingers with the jam and place them in a large glass dish. Sprinkle with the 18 Carat wine, the almonds and the lemon zest.

Make the custard to the recipe and strain it over the sponge fingers. Leave to cool.

Whip the cream until it is stiff and spread over the cold custard. Decorate with the crushed almonds and glacé cherries.

traditional custard sauce

This sauce is highly adaptable: for a Christmas brandy sauce omit the vanilla essence and add 3 tablespoons of brandy; for whisky or rum custard simply add 4 tablespoons of your favourite tipple at the end of cooking and whisk gently before serving.

It is easy to forget the simple things in life!

Makes 500 ml/17 fl. oz

2 free-range egg yolks
50 g/2 oz castor sugar
3 drops of vanilla essence
300 ml/½ pt milk
3 tbsp double cream

Heat the milk in a saucepan. Mix the yolks, sugar and vanilla essence in a large clean bowl. Gradually whisk in the hot milk. Return the custard to the saucepan and reheat, stirring all the time with a wooden spoon on a very low heat until it is thick enough to coat the back of the spoon.

Do not boil or the eggs will scramble.

While the custard is still warm, stir in the double cream.

drambuie custard tart

I was once asked in an interview during The Best of British, a cookery demonstration which takes place every year at Harrods, what my favourite British dessert was: this is number one, closely followed by clootie dumpling and sticky toffee pudding.

This Drambuie custard tart comes from my mother's recipe collection. Having tasted it all my life, I am sure once you have tried it, you will realise why she always made two at a time! The rich shortcrust pastry helps the flavour of the Drambuie custard and is very simple to make.

Essential ingredients are free-range eggs, best butter, heather honey and fresh full-cream milk. Do not cheat when making quality food.

Makes 2 x 18 cm/7 in. tarts

rich shortcrust pastry (see p. 139)
6 large free-range eggs
100 ml/4 fl. oz heather honey
300 ml/½ pt full-cream milk
200 ml/8 fl. oz double cream
60 ml/2 fl. oz Drambuie
freshly grated nutmeg

Make up the pastry.

Preheat the oven 200°C/400°F/Gas Mark 6.

Butter two 18 cm/7 in. flan rings on two non-stick baking trays and line the rings with cooking foil.

Roll the pastry out on a floured surface and leave to relax for 10 minutes before lining the flan rings with it.

Place the eggs and honey in a bowl and blend together. Heat the milk, cream and Drambuie, bring gently to the boil and remove from the heat. Allow this mixture to cool slightly, then pour it gently into the eggs and whisk thoroughly.

Distribute the filling evenly between the pastry cases. Grate a little nutmeg over the top of the custards, place in the oven and bake for 8 minutes.

Lower the heat to 150°C/300°F/Gas Mark 2 and bake for a further 20 minutes until the custards are set.

Let the tarts stand for 15 minutes, then carefully remove the flan ring and serve.

gateau of scottish strawberries, poached meringue, lemon shortbread and a strawberry sorbet

Jeff Bland, executive chef at the Balmoral Hotel in Edinburgh, was kind enough to send me this recipe, which I have adapted for the home cook.

Serves 4

16 Scottish strawberries
1 tbsp good-quality balsamic vinegar
50 g/2 oz chopped pistachios

FOR THE STRAWBERRY SORBET:
450 g/1 lb strawberries, hulled and washed
425 ml/¾ pt water
200 g/7 oz granulated sugar
zest and juice of 1 lemon

FOR THE LEMON SHORTBREAD:
250 g/9 oz plain flour, sieved
200 g/7 oz unsalted butter
100 g/4 oz icing sugar
zest of 1 lemon, finely grated
pinch salt
2 free-range egg yolks

FOR THE MERINGUES:
2 large free-range egg whites
100 g/4 oz castor sugar

Begin by making the strawberry sorbet. Put the water and sugar in a saucepan, stir and bring to the boil, adding the lemon zest as the mixture heats up. Once it has reached boiling point, leave the syrup to bubble for 2 minutes. Add the lemon juice, stir, pour into a plastic container and leave to cool completely. Meanwhile, liquidise the strawberries and rub the purée through a fine sieve. Reserve a few tablespoons of this to use to decorate the finished dish. Mix the purée with 125 ml/4½ fl. oz of the syrup, place in a plastic container and freeze for 4 hours. Every hour or so, remove from the freezer and beat the mixture thoroughly to break up large ice crystals and introduce some air into the sorbet.

Now make the lemon shortbread. Preheat the oven to 150°C/300°F/Gas Mark 2. Lightly cream the butter and icing sugar together, add lemon zest and salt. Mix in the yolks, lightly mix in the flour. Leave the dough to rest in refrigerator for half an hour. Cut out 8 biscuits of 5 inches in diameter, sit on a baking tray which has been greased and lined with baking paper, and place in the oven for 12 minutes.

For the meringues, place the egg whites in a large bowl and whisk until they are glossy and form stiff peaks, then add the sugar, approximately 25 g/1 oz at a time, whisking after each addition. Bring a large pan of boiling water to the simmer. Take a metal tablespoon and carefully drop spoons of the egg-white mixture into the hot water. Poach the meringues for 4 minutes, remove carefully onto greaseproof paper and place to one side until required.

Slice the strawberries and arrange in layers with the shortbread, topping with a poached meringue.

Top each gateau with a ball of strawberry sorbet.

Spoon around the vinegar, the reserved strawberry purée and the chopped pistachios.

macallan marmalade
roly-poly pudding

Macallan marmalade can be bought in most delicatessens and in Jenners and Harvey Nichols food halls. The possibilities for this recipe are endless, however. You could use any jam or fruit purée as a filling, or try it with dried fruits soaked in your favourite liqueur.

Serves 4

300 g/11 oz plain flour
1 tsp baking powder
150 g/5 oz shredded suet
300 g/11 oz Macallan whisky marmalade

Preheat the oven to 190°C/375°F/Gas Mark 5.

Sift the flour and baking powder into a bowl. Add the suet and a little cold water to make a soft dough. On a floured surface, roll the dough out into a rectangle about 5 mm/¼ in. thick.

Spread the marmalade almost to the edge of the pastry then dampen the edges of the pastry with a little milk or water, and roll up like a Swiss roll. Seal the edges at both ends so that the filling does not escape as it cooks.

Lightly grease a non-stick baking tray, sit the roly-poly on the tray, cover very loosely with greased greaseproof paper or greased baking foil and bake in the centre of the oven for 50 minutes.

Carefully remove the roly-poly from the oven, take off the paper or foil and trim the sealed edges so that the pudding has a nice Swiss-roll shape. Place on a warm plate and serve with warmed heather honey.

rice pie

These pies were sold in the streets during the early eighteenth century and apparently originated in the dock areas of Scotland when cargoes of rice were being shipped around the world.

Serves 4

rich shortcrust pastry (see p. 139)
110 g/4 oz short-grain rice
570 ml/1 pt milk
50 g/2 oz butter
75 g/3 oz castor sugar
275 ml/½ pt double cream
3 free-range eggs, well beaten
zest of ½ lemon, grated
freshly grated nutmeg
4 tbsp strawberry jam

Make up the pastry and roll it out.

Preheat the oven to 220°C/425°F/Gas Mark 8.

Put the rice in a saucepan, add the milk and bring slowly to just simmering point. Let it cook for 10 minutes. Remove the pan from the heat and add the butter, sugar and cream. Let the mixture cool for 2 minutes then add the eggs and lemon zest and place to one side.

Lightly butter a rimmed pie dish with a capacity of about 845 ml/1 ½ pt and line with the pastry. Coat the base with the strawberry jam. Pour over the rice pudding mixture, sprinkle with grated nutmeg and bake in the centre of the oven for 30 minutes.

Allow the pie to cool completely, chill for 2 hours in the fridge and serve with double cream or ice cream.

bread and butter pudding

For a delicious variation on this recipe, spread your favourite jam or marmalade on the bread after you butter it. Use half milk and half cream if you want an extra-rich pudding.

Serves 4

100 g/4 oz butter, softened
12 slices of thickly sliced white
    bread, crusts removed
175 g/6 oz sultanas
freshly grated nutmeg
400 ml/14 fl. oz milk
2 large free-range eggs
25 g/1 oz brown sugar
25 g/1 oz granulated sugar

Butter a 2-litre/4-pint pie dish. Butter the bread, cut into triangles and arrange in layers, butter side up. Sprinkle each layer with sultanas and grated nutmeg.

Heat the milk in a saucepan but do not let it boil. Place the eggs in a bowl with the brown sugar, beat with a whisk and slowly add the hot milk. Pour the egg mixture over the bread, sprinkle with the granulated sugar and more grated nutmeg, and leave to stand for 45 minutes.

Preheat the oven to 180°C/350°F/Gas Mark 4. Bake in the centre of the oven for 40 minutes until the custard is set.

icky sticky toffee pudding

If you're on a diet – tough!
   Serves 4

FOR THE PUDDING:
175 g/6 oz chopped dates
300 ml/½ pt water
1 tsp bicarbonate of soda
50 g/2 oz butter
175 g/6 oz sugar
2 free-range eggs, beaten
175 g/6 oz self-raising flour
vanilla essence

FOR THE SAUCE:
1 pt double cream
75 g/3 oz demerara sugar
1 tbsp black treacle

Preheat the oven to 180°C/350°F/Gas Mark 4.
   Boil the dates in the water with the bicarbonate of soda for 5 minutes.
   Mix all the other pudding ingredients together, then add the dates with their cooking liquid and stir well.
   Pour the mixture into a greased baking tin and bake for 45 minutes.
   Make the sauce by putting all the ingredients into a saucepan and boiling for 10 minutes.
   Pour the sauce over the sponge, place under the grill until it bubbles and serve.

steamed puddings

The recipes which follow are all for steamed puddings – the perfect warming, filling desserts for cold Scottish winter evenings.

The most characteristically Scottish of these is without doubt the clootie dumpling, which, rather than being cooked in a pudding basin, is boiled in a floured muslin cloth or 'cloot' – hence the name. It was traditionally a celebratory dish, served on New Year and birthdays, when trinkets or coins would be wrapped in greaseproof paper and included in the mix.

I first tasted this moist, lightly spiced fruit pudding while staying at Kinloch Lodge in Sleat on Skye. The ancestral home of the high chief of Clan Donald, it is now run as a small hotel and restaurant.

The recipe below was given to me by my friend Bob Herron, who comes from Fife and now lives in the village of Newburgh, Lancashire. Thanks, Bob. He and his wife Ann really do enjoy making this recipe. He told me that the Scottish paper the *Sunday Post* ran a Clootie Dumpling Contest and the winner was a Mrs J. Baird of Howgate in Penicuik. Her recipe bcame so popular that it is served all over Scotland.

Should you want to send Scotland's favourite pudding to some friends or family, the finest producers of this classic are Bill and Jill Adron at Tilquhillie Puddings in Banchory, who can be found in the Recommended Suppliers section at the back of the book.

clootie dumpling

It is important here that you purchase a large (at least 35 cm/14 in. square) piece of muslin – the cloot.

I like to serve mine with a hot sweet whisky sauce (see facing page) in winter or clotted cream in summer.

Serves 4

75 g/3 oz breadcrumbs
75 g/3 oz plain flour
75 g/3 oz shredded beef suet
50 g/2 oz soft brown sugar
75 g/3 oz sultanas
50 g/2 oz currants
2 tbsp golden syrup
I tsp ground cinnamon
I tsp ground ginger
freshly grated nutmeg
½ tsp baking soda
125 ml/4 fl. oz buttermilk
3 tbsp malt whisky

Mix all the ingredients except the buttermilk and whisky together in a large bowl. Add the buttermilk gradually, mixing well, until the mixture has a fairly soft consistency. Then blend in the whisky.

Run the cloot under hot water until it is warm and then wring it out.

Spread out the cloot and sprinkle with a thick layer of flour. Spread the cloot inside a large bowl and pour the mixture onto the cloot. Draw the corners of the cloot together and tie them up securely with string, allowing room for the dumpling to expand within the cloot.

Put an old plate upside down in a pan of boiling water. Place the dumpling on the plate and simmer for 3 hours, adding more boiling water as required.

Lift the dumpling out of the pan and put into a colander in the sink for a few minutes to allow the excess water to drain from the cloot. Untie the string and gently pull the corners of the cloot apart to display the clootie dumpling. Place on a large serving dish and taste something extra-special.

ayrshire pudding with a creamy whisky sauce

Ayrshire is an area well worth visiting for a very long weekend, with fantastic tourist attractions such as Culzean Castle and Country Park and great golf courses including Royal Troon, Prestwick and Turnberry. It was during the 1977 Open Championship at the latter that I first made and served this recipe – hence the name.

Serves 4

25 g/1 oz butter
50 g/2 oz glacé cherries, halved
100 g/4 oz raisins
100 g/4 oz white breadcrumbs
100 g/4 oz shredded suet
25 g/1 oz ground rice
100 g/4 oz castor sugar
zest of 1 lemon, grated
pinch salt
2 tbsp marmalade
2 free-range eggs, beaten
5 tbsp milk

FOR THE CREAMY WHISKY SAUCE:
50 g/2 oz butter
50 g/2 oz plain flour
300 ml/½ pt full-fat milk
50 g/2 oz castor sugar
100 ml/3 fl. oz double cream
4 tbsp single malt whisky
freshly grated nutmeg

Grease a 1-litre/2-pint pudding basin with the butter and line the base with half of the glacé cherries and some raisins, to decorate the top of the pudding.

In a bowl, mix together the rest of the cherries and raisins, the breadcrumbs, suet, rice, sugar, lemon zest, salt and marmalade. Mix the beaten egg with the milk and add to the other ingredients to form a soft paste mixture. Spoon this into the pudding basin, cover with greaseproof paper or cooking foil and secure with string.

Place the basin in a pan half filled with boiling water, cover with a tight-fitting lid and steam for 2½ hours.

When the pudding is about half an hour away from being ready, make the sauce: slowly melt the butter in a saucepan. Gently warm the milk in another saucepan. Work the flour into the melted butter using a wooden spoon. Cook the mixture, stirring, for 2 minutes.

Gradually add the warm milk. Blend in the sugar and cream. Whisk and cook on a low heat for 8 minutes. Add the whisky. Keep warm and just before serving grate in a little fresh nutmeg.

When the cooking time is over, remove the pudding basin from the pan and let it stand for 10 minutes, then turn the pudding out onto a warm serving plate and pour over the creamy whisky sauce.

heather honey pudding

This recipe is also delicious made with marmalade or jam.

Serves 4

200 g/7 oz heather honey
75 g/3 oz breadcrumbs
zest of 1 lemon, grated

FOR THE SUET CRUST:
300 g/11 oz plain flour
pinch salt
2 tsp baking powder
150 g/3 oz shredded suet
approx. 250 ml/8 fl. oz cold water

Lightly grease a 1-litre/2-pint pudding basin and half-fill a large saucepan with a tight-fitting lid with boiling water.

To make the pastry, sift the flour, salt and baking powder into a clean, dry mixing bowl. Add the suet and enough water to make a dough.

Divide the dough into two on a floured surface. Roll out the first portion to make a circle 1 cm/$\frac{1}{2}$ in. larger than the top of the pudding basin.

Lay the pastry in the basin and mould it all around the inside of the basin, easing it evenly up the sides to the top.

Use the remaining portion of pastry to make a lid to fit the top of the basin and two rounds to fit the basin at two levels.

Spread a generous layer of marmalade onto the base of the pudding, cover with a layer of the breadcrumbs and lemon rind, top with a pastry round and repeat the process until all the ingredients are used, finishing with the pastry lid.

Cover the pudding with greaseproof paper or cooking foil and secure with string. Place the pudding in the saucepan with the boiling water, cover and steam for 2$\frac{1}{2}$ hours.

Leave for 10 minutes to stand and then very carefully turn the pudding out onto a warm serving plate and serve with double cream or vanilla ice cream.

seed steamed pudding

This is a traditional recipe dating back to the seventeenth century, when currants were known as 'seed'.

Serves 4

125 g/5 oz currants
400 ml/14 fl. oz milk
3 large free-range eggs
2 tbsp heather honey
25 g/1 oz castor sugar
1 tsp freshly grated lemon zest
4 slices white bread, crusts removed and cut into 5 mm/⅓ in. square pieces

Lightly butter a 1-litre/2-pint pudding basin and firmly press 25 g/1 oz of the currants onto the base and sides of the basin to decorate the pudding.

Gently heat the milk but do not let it boil. Mix together the eggs, honey and sugar in another bowl, add the milk, the remaining currants and the lemon zest. Put the pieces of bread in a bowl. Pour the mixture over the bread and leave to stand for 15 minutes.

Pour the bread mixture into the pudding basin, cover with greaseproof paper or buttered cooking foil and secure with string.

Place the basin in a saucepan half-filled with boiling water, cover with a lid and steam gently for 80 minutes, topping up with water if necessary.

Remove the pudding and allow it to stand for 5 minutes, then turn out and serve with custard sauce (see p. 173).

the helen atkinson chocolate pudding

I write a cookery column in the north of England for a group of newspapers. Food-lovers write in requesting various recipes; once a month I get a request for a chocolate recipe and it comes from the same person every time. Helen Atkinson is a chocolate fanatic. The annoying thing is, she is not fat – there is more fat on a chip. She loves chocolate so much, they should have named a chocolate pudding after her and with that in mind, I decided to create one. Use only the best-quality chocolate and, with the Grand Marnier liqueur, you will have the ultimate chocolate pudding.

Serves 4

125 g/5 oz plain chocolate, grated
250 ml/8 fl. oz fresh milk
1 tbsp heather honey
3 tbsp Grand Marnier
100 g/4 oz butter
100 g/4 oz castor sugar
4 free-range eggs, separated
225 g/8 oz white breadcrumbs
½ tsp baking powder

Butter the inside of a 2-litre/4-pint pudding basin.

Gently heat the grated chocolate and milk in a saucepan until the chocolate dissolves. Add the honey and Grand Marnier and blend them in.

Place the butter and sugar in a bowl and cream them together. Beat in the egg yolks and add the melted chocolate mixture. Stir in the breadcrumbs and the baking powder.

In a separate bowl, whisk the egg whites until they are stiff. Carefully fold them into the pudding mixture.

Spoon the mixture into the greased pudding basin and cover with greaseproof paper or cooking foil, securing with string. Put the basin in a pan half-filled with boiling water, place on a tight-fitting lid and gently simmer for 2 hours.

Let the pudding stand for 10 minutes, then carefully turn it out onto a warm plate. Serve with a rich chocolate sauce and top with vanilla ice cream.

bread, biscuits and cakes

I remember coming home from junior school with my brother Jim and sister Marie to the heavenly smell of home-made bread; it just lingered around the house for hours and with my mother taking the hot gingerbread from the oven it was like living in a bakery. From a very young age, I was intrigued by food and enjoyed the experience of making scones and baking bread, cakes and pies. That to me is what home is all about: the smells of the old family recipes from the past coming back to life.

With that in mind, I wanted to find the most traditional bread, cake and biscuit recipes from the hearth and home of Scotland for this chapter – classics like rustic white cottage loaf, fruit bread, whisky loaf, Dundee cake, tablet and black bun, to name but a few. These recipes are timeless and now make guest appearances in the bakery sections of supermarkets across the country. But I say it again: there is nothing nicer than the smell and taste of warm home baking fresh from the oven.

When kneading dough, first stretch it away from you, then gather it back into a ball. Give the dough a quarter-turn and repeat the process until it changes texture to become smooth and elastic.

When you take a fresh loaf out of the oven, to test that is completely baked, give it a tap on the base – it should make a hollow sound. Leave it to cool naturally on a wire rack.

rustic white cottage loaf with heather honey and sesame seeds

This is one of my own favourite recipes. Because I live in a cottage, really all the loaves that come out of my oven are cottage loaves!

You can also use this recipe to make ordinary loaf-shaped crusty bread by using 2 x 450 g/ 1 lb bread tins and dividing the dough between them.

For a fruitier loaf, add 75 g/3 oz sultanas with 1 teaspoon of cinnamon to the dry ingredients.

450 g/1 lb strong white flour
1 tsp salt
7 g/⅓ oz lard
7 g/⅓ oz yeast
450 ml/¾ pt warm water
2 tbsp heather honey
1 tbsp sesame seeds

Sieve the flour and salt into a mixing bowl and rub in the lard. Mix the yeast with 1 tablespoon of the warm water and add to the rest of the water, stirring well. Add this to the flour, ensuring it is fully blended. Turn the dough out onto a lightly floured surface and knead until it becomes smooth and elastic. Shape into a ball, place in a warm greased bowl, cover with greased clingfilm and leave in a warm area to rise for 2 hours, until it has doubled in size.

Turn the dough out onto a lightly floured surface and really press it out with the ball of your hand for 3 minutes. Shape it back into a ball again, put it back in the bowl, cover with greased clingfilm and return to a warm area for a further hour.

Lightly butter a baking tray.

Cut off just over one-third of the dough and shape the pieces into a large and a small ball. Moisten the top of the large ball and place the small one on top of it. Sit the loaf on the greased baking tray. Hold the first three fingers of both hands together and push them down into the top ball until you reach the larger ball, sealing the two parts together. Cover with greased clingfilm and leave to rise for 40 minutes in a warm area.

Preheat the oven to 220°C/425°F/Gas Mark 8.

Bake in the centre of the oven for 35 minutes. Coat the top of the bread with the honey, sprinkle with the sesame seeds and bake for a further 10 minutes.

small breakfast loaves

Makes 8–10

> 900 g/2 lb fine wheat flour
> 1 tsp salt
> 50 g/2 oz butter
> 25 g/1 oz fresh yeast
> 1 tbsp sugar
> 600 ml/1 pt milk, warmed
> 1 free-range egg, beaten

Mix the flour and salt in a large bowl and rub in the butter. Mix the yeast to a paste with the sugar and 3 tablespoons of the warm milk. Add the yeast to the rest of the milk with the beaten egg.

Make a well in centre of the flour and pour in the yeast mixture, blending thoroughly into a dough.

Turn the dough out onto a lightly floured surface and knead until it becomes smooth and elastic. Shape into individual small flat round cakes about 2.5 cm/1 in. thick and 7 cm/3 in. in diameter. Mark them with a palette knife, making diamond-shaped incisions about 2.5 cm/ 1 in. in length.

Place them on a greased baking tray, cover with clingfilm and leave in a warm place for 40 minutes.

Preheat the oven to 200°C/400°F/Gas Mark 6.

Remove the clingfilm and bake in the centre of the oven for 20 minutes.

black-pudding bread

This bread makes a delicious crispy bacon and corn-fed chicken sandwich with a little HP sauce. Or try it fried with runny eggs for your breakfast.

You can use this recipe to make two loaves, rather than one cottage loaf, by dividing the dough between two 450 g/1 lb bread tins.

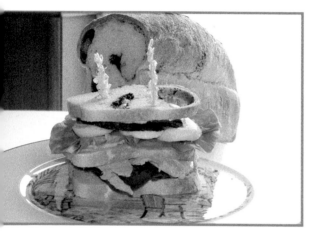

450 g/1 lb strong white flour
1 tsp salt
7 g/⅓ oz lard
7 g/⅓ oz yeast
450 ml/¾ pt warm water
100 g/4 oz black pudding, crumbled
1 tbsp honey
1 tbsp sesame seeds

Sieve the flour and salt into a mixing bowl and rub in the lard. Mix the yeast with 1 tablespoon of the warm water and add to the rest of the water, stirring well. Add this to the flour, ensuring it is fully blended. Turn the dough out onto a lightly floured surface and knead until it becomes smooth and elastic. Shape into a ball, place in a warm greased bowl, cover with greased clingfilm and leave in a warm area to rise for 2 hours, until it has doubled in size.

Turn the dough out onto a lightly floured surface and really press it out with the ball of your hand for 3 minutes. Add the crumbled black pudding to the mixture and shape it into a ball again. Put it back in the bowl, cover with greased clingfilm and return to a warm area for a further hour.

Lightly butter a baking tray.

Cut off just over one-third of the dough and shape the pieces into a large and a small ball. Moisten the top of the large ball and place the small one on top of it. Sit the loaf on the greased baking tray. Hold the first three fingers of both hands together and push them down into the top ball until you reach the larger ball, sealing the two parts together. Cover with greased clingfilm and leave to rise for 40 minutes in a warm area.

Preheat the oven to 220°C/425°F/Gas Mark 8.

Bake in the centre of the oven for 35 minutes. Coat the top of the bread with the honey, sprinkle with the sesame seeds and bake for a further 10 minutes.

brown bread

450 g/1 lb wholemeal flour
1 tsp salt
7 g/⅓ oz lard, softened
1 tsp soft brown sugar
300 ml/½ pt milk, warmed
15 g/½ oz fresh yeast

FOR THE GLAZE:
1 tbsp honey, warmed
1 tbsp wholemeal flour
1 tbsp poppy seeds

Place the wholemeal flour and salt in a bowl and gently rub in the lard. Make a well in the centre of the mixture. Add the sugar to the warm milk and whisk until dissolved. Use 2 tablespoons of the milk to mix the yeast to a paste, add the rest of the milk to the yeast and pour into the well. Blend the mixture thoroughly. Turn the dough out onto a lightly floured surface and knead until it becomes smooth and elastic. Shape into a ball and put in a greased bowl, cover with clingfilm and leave in a warm place to rise for 60 minutes.

Flour your work surface with wholemeal flour and knead the dough, working out the air, for 2 minutes.

Place the dough in a greased loaf tin, cover with clingfilm and leave in a warm place for 30 minutes.

Preheat the oven to 220°C/425°F/Gas Mark 8.

Remove the clingfilm, place in the centre of the oven and bake for 30 minutes.

Brush the top lightly with honey, sprinkle with the wholemeal flour and poppy seeds, and return to the oven for a further 10 minutes.

cameron house heather honey and walnut bread

Simon Whitley, the chef at Cameron House, makes this heather honey and walnut bread for the restaurants there. It became so popular that he now makes the bread for all the guest-lodge owners on Loch Lomond. We have some friends from Northern Ireland who come to stay with us at our lodge every year and they always bring Jayne and me plenty of Irish butter. Top that with Scottish cheddar and you have a great combination, believe me!

    450 g/1 lb strong white flour
    1 tsp salt
    7 g/⅓ oz lard
    7 g/⅓ oz yeast
    450 ml/¾ pt warm water
    50 g/2 oz walnuts
    3 tbsp heather honey, warmed

Sieve the flour and salt into a mixing bowl and rub in the lard. Mix the yeast with 1 tablespoon of the warm water and add to the rest of the water, stirring well. Add this to the flour, ensuring it is fully blended. Turn the dough out onto a lightly floured surface and knead until it becomes smooth and elastic. Shape into a ball, place in a warm greased bowl, cover with greased clingfilm and leave in a warm area to rise for 2 hours, until it has doubled in size.

Turn the dough out onto a lightly floured surface and really press it out with the ball of your hand for 3 minutes. Add the walnuts to the mixture and shape it into a ball again. Put it back in the bowl, cover with greased clingfilm and return to a warm area for a further hour.

Lightly butter a baking tray.

Cut off just over one-third of the dough and shape the pieces into a large and a small ball. Moisten the top of the large ball and place the small one on top of it. Sit the loaf on the greased baking tray. Hold the first three fingers of both hands together and push them down into the top ball until you reach the larger ball, sealing the two parts together. Cover with greased clingfilm and leave to rise for 40 minutes in a warm area.

Preheat the oven to 220°C/425°F/Gas Mark 8.

Bake in the centre of the oven for 35 minutes. Remove and spread with the honey, then return to the oven for a further 10 minutes.

traditional scottish oatcakes

These were served to the Young Pretender's soldiers after the battle of Culloden in 1746, so perhaps they should really be called Bonnie Prince Charlie Oatcakes.

I make this recipe on every visit to the lodge Jayne and I have at Loch Lomond, to complement either a Dunlop cheese or my homemade Loch Fyne kipper paste (see p. 52). They also go well with potted cheese recipes such as that on p. 51.

Makes 8

225 g/8 oz fine oatmeal
25 g/1 oz soft brown sugar
½ tsp baking powder
pinch salt
25 g/1 oz butter
150 ml/⅓ pt boiling water

Preheat the oven to 190°C/375°F/Gas Mark 5.

Put the oatmeal, sugar, baking powder and salt into a bowl and mix them thoroughly. Melt the butter in the boiling water and pour this over the dry ingredients, blending well.

Dust your hands with oatmeal and form the dough into a ball.

Place the mixture on a surface sprinkled with oatmeal and roll out as thinly as you possibly can. Using a pastry cutter, cut the dough into rounds and place them on a greased baking tray.

Bake in the centre of the oven for 20 minutes. Allow to cool and serve with butter.

selkirk bannock

Robbie Douglas introduced the Selkirk bannock in the mid-nineteenth century from his wee shop in the marketplace of the Borders town. It was traditionally served during the bride's breakfast, on the first day of summer and on May Day.

Makes 2

450 g/1 lb strong white flour
1 tsp salt
75 g/3 oz butter
75 g/3 oz sugar
300 ml/10 fl. oz milk, warmed
25 g/1 oz fresh yeast
450 g/1 lb sultanas
1 free-range egg, beaten

Sieve the flour and salt into a large mixing bowl and roughly rub in the butter. Add the sugar to the milk. Blend 3 tablespoons of the milk with the yeast in a large bowl and slowly add the rest of the milk. Add the yeast and milk to the flour and butter and mix thoroughly to form a dough. Turn the dough out onto a lightly floured surface and knead until it becomes smooth and elastic. Shape the dough into a ball, cover with clingfilm and place in a warm area to rise for 25 minutes.

Knead in the sultanas and leave to stand for 20 minutes.

Divide the dough into two equal pieces and mould each piece into a ball. Place onto two baking trays, cover again with clingfilm and leave in a warm area for 40 minutes.

Preheat the oven to 200°C/400°F/Gas Mark 6.

Remove the clingfilm, flatten each ball of dough so that they resemble flat cakes and brush lightly with the beaten egg. Bake in the centre of the oven for 20 minutes.

scotch cakes

I got this recipe from my 1861 *Mrs Beeton's Household Management*; it is simple and tastes great. Here is her original recipe – have a go and see if you can make it.

INGREDIENTS for a dozen cakes – 1½ lb of flour, ¾ lb of butter, ¾ lb of sugar, 2 tablespoonfuls of ground caraway seeds, ½ that quantity of cinnamon, a little citron or other candied-peel, cut in small slices. AVERAGE COST, 1s, 6d.

Cream the butter; add the sugar, then slowly the flour; then the flavouring and the citron. Butter some patty pans and put the mixture in, and bake for 15 minutes.

scottish fruit buns

When baking, remember that yeast is an organism that needs moisture, warmth, and flour or sugar to stimulate its growth. As it ferments, it produces carbon dioxide, which makes the dough rise. According to my dear friend and fellow chef Barry Rea, who serves his freshly baked fruit rolls straight from the oven when the cheese course is being placed on the table, 'Fresh yeast is far better and easier to use than dry yeast and gives the fruit buns a much fuller flavour.'

Makes 12

FOR THE FERMENT:
1 large free-range egg, beaten
150 ml/¼ pt milk, warmed
1 tbsp sugar
20 g/¾ oz fresh yeast
50 g/2 oz strong white flour

FOR THE GLAZE:
1 free-range egg, beaten
25 g/1 oz crystallised sugar

FOR THE DOUGH:
450 g/1 lb strong white flour
175 g/6 oz softened butter
1 free-range egg, beaten
175 g/6 oz crystallised sugar
50 g/2 oz sultanas
50 g/2 oz currants
50 g/2 oz candied citrus peel, chopped
zest of 1 lemon, finely grated

To prepare the ferment, stir the beaten egg into the warm milk, add the sugar and use 3 tablespoons of the warm milk to blend the yeast to a smooth paste in a large bowl. Add the remaining milk and whisk in the flour to make a batter. Cover the bowl with clingfilm and leave in a warm place for 30 minutes.

Blend together the flour, butter and egg, and add to the ferment, kneading the mixture on a lightly floured surface until it becomes smooth and elastic. Cover with clingfilm and leave for 60 minutes.

Put the mixture in a bowl and add the sugar, sultanas, currants, peel and grated lemon rind, blend mix together and leave for 5 minutes.

Using a tablespoon, place small mounds of the bun mixture onto two greased baking trays, cover with clingfilm and leave to rise for a further 25 minutes.

Preheat the oven to 220°C/425°F/Gas Mark 8.

Brush the buns lightly with the beaten egg, sprinkle with the sugar and bake in the centre of the oven for 20 minutes until golden brown.

Allow them to cool slightly and then serve warm with lashings of butter.

whisky loaf

One of Scotland's most popular exports is without doubt whisky and the reason is simple: no one else makes whisky like the distilleries of Scotland. I think it's important to try to use the best-quality ingredients when baking and as *Whisky Magazine* recently awarded Macallan four of the top ten places in their list of the ninety best Scotch whiskies in the world, including the number-one position, I always use a Macallan Fine Oak when making my whisky cakes.

Serve this with lashings of butter, a really high-quality robust cheese and a wee dram.

275 g/10 oz strong white flour
1 tsp salt
25 g/1 oz lard
25 g/1 oz soft brown sugar
1 level tsp ground mixed spice
1 large free-range egg, beaten
150 ml/¼ pt warm water

50 ml/2 fl. oz single-malt whisky
25 g/1 oz fresh yeast
225 g/8 oz currants
100 g/4 oz sultanas
1 tbsp apricot jam
1 tbsp poppy seeds

Lightly butter a 900 g/2 lb loaf tin or two 450 g/1 lb loaf tins.

Sieve the flour and salt into a large mixing bowl, add the lard and rub it into the flour. Add the sugar and spice, mixing again, and make a well in the centre of the mixture.

Blend the egg with the warm water. Use 2 tablespoons of this to make a smooth paste with the yeast and then blend the paste back into the water. Add the whisky and pour the liquid into the well in the flour, mixing thoroughly and vigorously.

Knead until the dough has a smooth, elastic consistency. Add the currants and sultanas, kneading them into the dough.

Roll into an oblong shape to fit the loaf tin or divide to fit the 2 tins.

Place the tin on a baking tray, cover with greased clingfilm and put in a warm place for 2 hours.

Preheat the oven to 180°C/350°F/Gas Mark 4.

Remove the clingfilm and bake in the centre of the oven for 30 minutes. Remove from the oven, spread the jam over the top and sprinkle with the poppy seeds. Bake for a further 10 minutes and allow to rest for 1 hour before serving.

scottish parkin

Parkin is a traditional type of gingerbread made with oatmeal. Scottish parkin uses heather honey and whisky, and is lighter than the Yorkshire or Lancashire version. I suggest trying this recipe with a selection of Scottish cheeses, such as Dunlop, Orkney and Mull.

225 g/8 oz plain flour, sifted
2 tsp baking powder
225 g/8 oz oatmeal
2 tsp ground ginger
pinch salt
50 g/2 oz brown sugar
freshly grated nutmeg
pinch bicarbonate of soda
225 g/6 oz heather honey
100 g/4 oz butter
2 tbsp whisky
75 ml/2 fl. oz milk

Preheat the oven to 150°C/300°F/Gas Mark 2.

In a large bowl, lightly mix the flour, baking powder, oatmeal, ginger, salt, sugar, nutmeg and bicarbonate of soda.

Gently heat the honey and butter in a saucepan. Add this to the dry ingredients and then gradually mix in the whisky and milk.

Line a loaf tin with greaseproof paper and pour in the mixture.

Bake in the centre of the oven for 45 minutes.

Leave the parkin for 24 hours to cool completely.

maids of honour

These are well known in all the tearooms throughout Great Britain.
Makes 12

175 g/6 oz shortcrust pastry (see p. 139)
25 g/1 oz butter
150 ml/⅓ pt milk
25 g/1 oz cake crumbs
50 g/2 oz butter, cut into small pieces
25 g/1 oz castor sugar
50 g/2 oz ground almonds
1 free-range egg, beaten
zest of 1 lemon, grated
½ tsp almond essence
4 tbsp strawberry jam

Make the pastry.

Preheat the oven to 220°C/425°F/Gas Mark 8.

Butter a 12-cake patty tray.

Gently heat the milk in a saucepan but do not boil. Add the cake crumbs, butter, sugar, ground almonds, egg, lemon zest and almond essence, stirring all the ingredients together. Leave to stand for 10 minutes.

Roll the pastry out and cut out 12 rounds using a fluted 7 cm/3 in. pastry cutter. Place the rounds in the tray and spread the base of each one generously with strawberry jam. Divide the filling mixture equally between the pastry cups.

Bake in the centre of the oven for 20 minutes until golden brown. Allow the maids of honour to cool for 5 minutes before removing them from the tray.

shortbread

No visit to Scotland would be complete without a tin of shortbread to take home and that tin is likely to be from Walkers, those fine makers of shortbread and oatcakes. Joseph Walker started his company as a village bakery in Aberlour-on-Spey in 1898. But the following shortbread recipe dates back even further, to 1800:

REAL SCOTCH SHORT BREAD

One pound of butter, two pounds of flour; half pound of sifted sugar; some sweet almonds; a few caraway comfits; and some citron.

Put a pound of butter into a basin, and squeeze it near the fire with the hand till quite soft; then squeeze into it two pounds of flour and half a pound of sifted loaf sugar with a few sweet almonds chopped very fine. Mix all well together. Take portions of it and shape into cakes of 1 cm/½ inch thick with the hand. Bake in a slow oven. To this may be added caraway comfits and citron.

Warnes Model Cookery, Mary Jewry, 1868

strawberry shortbread

If you can get hold of them, wild Scottish strawberries will make this recipe taste even better. For a more rustic-looking dessert, layer the shortbread as a single large cake, as in the photograph. A well-loved summer recipe, this should be served with champagne.

Serves 4

900 g/2 lb fresh strawberries, hulled and
  halved
150 ml/½ pt whisky

FOR THE SHORTBREAD:
225 g/8 oz plain flour
100 g/4 oz butter, softened
50 g/2 oz castor sugar
1 free-range egg, separated

FOR THE STRAWBERRY PURÉE:
2 tbsp double cream
1 tsp fresh lemon juice
1 tbsp castor sugar

FOR THE TOPPING:
425 ml/¾ pt double cream, whipped
icing sugar

Soak the strawberries in the whisky for 2 hours. Drain and place to one side.

Preheat the oven to 400°F/200°C/Gas Mark 6.

Put the flour and softened butter in a large bowl and gently rub the butter into the flour with your fingertips until the mixture resembles breadcrumbs. Add the sugar, blending thoroughly, and then add the egg yolk to bind the mixture together.

On a floured surface, flatten the mixture with your hands until it is about 5 mm/¼ in. thick. Prick the surface with a fork, then cut out 12 rounds with a 7.5 cm/3 in. fluted

cutter. Place the biscuits on a greased baking tray, brush lightly with the white of the egg and sprinkle with castor sugar.

Bake for 25 minutes, until they are a light golden brown. Transfer to a wire rack.

Meanwhile, make up the strawberry purée by taking 250 g/9 oz of the strawberries and putting them in a food processor or blender with the double cream, lemon juice and castor sugar. Chill the purée.

Place one biscuit in the centre of each plate and cover evenly with a layer of cream and a layer of sliced strawberries. Top with another biscuit and repeat the process, finishing off the third biscuit with a dusting of icing sugar. Garnish with a fan of strawberries, a little more cream and some strawberry purée.

chocolate-covered tablet

Tablet is immensely popular in Scotland. This traditional sweet lends itself to adaptation. You could add coconut or walnuts, a few drops of peppermint oil, lemon or orange juice or cinnamon. But for me, the most enjoyable variation is tablet coated in a good-quality milk chocolate. Heavenly with after-dinner drinks or coffee!

420 ml/14 fl. oz condensed milk
1 kg/2 lb granulated sugar
270 g/9 oz butter
600 ml/1 pt hot water
350 g/12 oz good-quality Swiss milk chocolate, broken into small pieces

Place all the ingredients except the chocolate in a large pan and bring to the boil. Turn down the heat and simmer for 30 minutes. Stir every 5 minutes. The tablet should develop a thick, gooey consistency, so stir with extra vigour towards the end of the 30 minutes.

Pour the tablet liquid into a 30 cm/12 in. x 24 cm/10 in. baking tray. Let it set for 12 minutes, then cut into bitesize squares. Leave to harden for a further 4 hours.

Slowly melt the chocolate in a heatproof bowl set over a saucepan of gently simmering water. Stir with a wooden spoon until completely melted. Allow the chocolate to cool slightly. When the tablet is completely set, dip the bitesize pieces in the chocolate to coat them completely. Alternatively, allow the tablet to harden completely before cutting it into squares, paint a thick strip of melted chocolate over it with a pastry brush, leave it to set in the fridge and then cut into bitesize pieces.

dundee cake

I really enjoy a slice of Dundee cake with a mature Dunlop cheese or a Mull of Kintyre cheddar.

175 g/6 oz butter
175 g/6 oz soft brown sugar
4 free-range eggs, beaten
225 g/8 oz plain flour, sifted
50 g/2 oz self-raising flour
25 g/1 oz ground almonds
25 g/1 oz blanched almonds, chopped
pinch salt
175 g/6 oz sultanas
100 g/4 oz currants
50 g/2 oz mixed peel
50 g/2 oz glacé cherries, chopped
zest of 1 lemon
zest of 1 orange
50 ml/2 fl. oz dry sherry
50 g/2 oz whole roasted almonds

Preheat the oven to 160°C/325°F/Gas Mark 3.

Cream the butter and sugar together for 3 minutes, beat in the eggs and fold in the flours, salt, and ground and chopped almonds, blending thoroughly. Add the rest of the ingredients except the whole almonds and blend thoroughly again.

Lightly butter a 20 cm/8 in. round cake tin and line it with a double layer of greaseproof paper.

Carefully spoon the cake mixture into the tin. Smooth the top and make a slight hollow in the centre. Arrange the whole roasted almonds on the surface of the cake in concentric circles.

Bake in the centre of the oven for 2 hours. Cover the top with greaseproof paper and bake for a further 45 minutes. Leave to cool in the tin for at least 45 minutes. Place on a wire rack for a further 45 minutes and then eat at your leisure.

morayshire gingerbread

There are many varieties of gingerbread in Scotland, with Morayshire having two very different versions. One, dating from the Victorian era, uses a teaspoon of bicarbonate of soda with a half-pint of beer. I have tried it but I found it very bitter. This recipe, however, uses rum, which gives it a lovely warm, rich taste.

225 g/8 oz self-raising flour
100 g/4 oz soft brown sugar
1 tbsp ground ginger
pinch salt
100 g/4 oz butter
1 large tbsp golden syrup
1 free-range egg, separated, plus one yolk
100 g/4 oz mixed peel
2 tbsp dark rum

FOR THE TOPPING:
2 tbsp soft brown sugar
1 tsp ginger

Preheat the oven to 160°C/325°F/Gas Mark 3.

Grease a 20 cm/8 in. x 10 cm/4 in. loaf tin.

Put the flour, sugar, ginger and salt in a bowl. Melt the butter and syrup in a saucepan over a low heat. Beat the egg yolks together. Take the pan from the heat and whisk in the egg yolks. Pour this mixture onto the dry ingredients, blending thoroughly.

Soak the mixed peel in the rum for 3 minutes.

Press half the gingerbread mixture into the tin, sprinkle with the rum-flavoured peel and top with the remaining mixture.

Lightly whisk the egg white and brush the top with it. Put the sugar and ginger into a plastic bag and shake together. Sprinkle this onto the surface of the gingerbread and bake in the centre of the oven for 30 to 35 minutes.

black bun

The following ode to black bun can be found in F. Marian McNeill's 1929 book *The Scots Kitchen*:

> Thou tuck-shop king! Joy of our gourmand youth!
> What days though mark'st and what blood-curdling nights,
> Nights full of shapeless things, hideous, uncouth;
> Imp follows ghoul, ghoul follows jinn, pell-mell;
> Fierce raisin-devils and gay currant sprites
> Hold lightsome leap-frog in a pastry hell.
>   Augustus Bejant, 'Invocation to Black Bun'

I first tasted black bun during one of my annual visits to Edinburgh with my wife Jayne. I tried it at the Farmers' Market that is held at Castle Terrace every Saturday morning. I then delved into the history of this tasty cake. Black bun, also known as Scotch bun, was always eaten on Twelfth Night and is now made for Hogmanay. It is very similar to Christmas cake except it is lined and topped with a short pastry and laced with a wee dram.

shortcrust pastry (see p. 139)
450 g/1 lb raisins
450 g/1 lb currants
50 g/2 oz blanched almonds, chopped
50 g/2 oz mixed peel
75 g/3 oz demerara sugar

150 g/6 oz plain flour
1 tsp ground cloves
1 tsp ground ginger
1 tsp ground allspice
generous pinch black pepper
½ tsp baking powder

Make the pastry.

Mix the raisins, currants, almonds, mixed peel and brown sugar together. Carefully sift in the flour and then add the cloves, ginger, allspice, black pepper and baking powder. Bind the mixture together using 1 of the eggs beaten with the whisky. Place the mixture to one side.

Lightly butter a 23 cm/9 in. cake tin and preheat the oven to 160°C/325°F/Gas Mark 3.

Roll out three-quarters of the pastry and line the sides and base of the tin.

Fill the lined tin with the black bun mixture and roll out the remaining dough to seal in the mixture, crimping the pastry edges together. Lightly prick the surface with a fork. Using a skewer, make 4 holes right to the bottom of the cake.

Brush with the remaining egg then bake in the centre of the oven for 3 hours.

Allow the black bun to cool and store it in an airtight tin until Hogmanay.

traditional cherry mince pies with whisky and almonds

The mincemeat can be made months before Christmas and stored in eight 450 g/1 lb preserving jars. You could decorate the jars with some Christmas wrapping paper and give them to your friends for presents.

I use Macallan single malt for this recipe; it is worth going for the highest quality ingredients for that special event that comes only once a year.

Makes 12

FOR THE MINCEMEAT:
450 g/1 lb glacé cherries, chopped
450 g/1 lb sultanas
450 g/1 lb raisins
450 g/1 lb currants
450 g/1 lb soft brown sugar
450 g/1 lb shredded beef suet
450 g/1 lb mixed peel
zest and juice of 3 lemons
450 g/1 lb apples, peeled, cored and diced small
225 g/8 oz blanched almonds, chopped
150 g/⅓ pt single malt whisky
1 tsp ground ginger
1 tsp ground cinnamon
freshly grated nutmeg

FOR THE CHRISTMAS SHORTCRUST PASTRY:
350 g/12 oz plain flour, sifted
½ tsp salt
75 g/3 oz butter
75 g/3 oz lard
25 g/1 oz castor sugar
25 g/1 oz ground almonds
3 tbsp cold water
1 free-range egg yolk
½ tsp almond essence
1 free-range egg, beaten with a little milk
icing sugar

For the mincemeat, simply mix all the ingredients together in a large bowl and leave to stand for 4 hours. Mix again and leave for a further 2 hours.

Divide between warm, sterilised jars (see p. 215). Place a circle of waxed or greaseproof paper on top of the mincemeat, seal with the lids and keep until required, adding a further 2 tablespoons of whisky after 6 weeks. The mincemeat should keep for up to three years and will mature over that period.

When you're ready to make the pies, sift the flour and salt into a clean bowl. Gently rub in the butter, lard, sugar and ground almonds until the mixture resembles fine breadcrumbs. Mix the cold water and the egg yolk and add to the other ingredients with a little almond essence. Mix the dough together with your fingertips.

Allow to rest for 45 minutes and then knead gently until soft.

Sprinkle the pastry with a little sifted flour and roll out on a lightly floured surface.

Preheat the oven to 190°C/375°F/Gas Mark 5.

Divide the pastry into two. Roll one half out to about 5 mm/¼ in., cut out rounds about 10 cm/4 in. in diameter and line a 12-tartlet baking tray with these. Fill each tartlet with enough of the cherry mincemeat to come 5 mm/¼ in. from the top.

Roll out the remaining pastry and cut out lids to fit the tarts. Dampen the edges of the pastry with the egg wash and press the lids down, sealing the edges. Cut a small V shape into each lid to allow the heat to escape.

Brush with the egg wash and bake for 20 minutes, until golden brown. Cool on a wire rack.

Sprinkle the pies with icing sugar and place in an airtight container, covering each layer with greaseproof paper. Store the container in a dark, dry cupboard until required. The pies will keep for two months.

the ultimate whisky christmas cake

Ensure you use a really good-quality whisky for this cake, as this is what will make it not just a good cake but a fantastic cake worthy of a special occasion.

175 g/6 oz currants
225 g/8 oz raisins
225 g/8 oz sultanas
100 g/4 oz glacé cherries, chopped
50 g/2 oz mixed peel
zest of 1 lemon
zest of 1 orange
125 ml/4 fl. oz single malt whisky
225 g/8 oz butter
225 g/8 oz soft brown sugar
½ tsp gravy browning
225 g/8 oz plain flour
½ tsp baking powder
pinch salt
1 tsp mixed spice
6 free-range eggs, beaten
100 g/4 oz blanched almonds, chopped
1 tbsp dark treacle, warmed
1 tsp freshly grated nutmeg

The night before you make the cake, put all the dried fruit and peel in a clean glass bowl and mix in the whisky. Cover and leave to stand for 24 hours.

Line a 25 cm/10 in. square or round cake tin with greaseproof paper.

Place the butter and sugar in a very large bowl and stir until they are completely blended. Add the gravy browning.

Sift the flour with the baking powder, salt and mixed spice. Alternate between adding small amounts of the flour mixture and the beaten eggs to the butter mixture, mixing thoroughly, until both ingredients are used up.

Add the rest of the ingredients and stir until everything is completely blended. Leave the mixture to settle for 1 hour.

Preheat the oven to 160°C/325°F/Gas Mark 3.

Give the mixture a final stir and put it into the cake tin. Cover the surface of the mixture with a piece of greaseproof paper.

Bake in the centre of the oven for 45 minutes then lower the heat to 140°C/275°F/Gas Mark 1 and cook for 4 hours.

Take the cake out of the oven and allow it to cool completely before you remove it from the tin. Discard the greaseproof paper. Turn the cake over and sprinkle the bottom with 4 tablespoons of whisky. Wrap the cake in a double layer of greaseproof paper, then in cooking foil. Place in a large container or biscuit tin and store in a cool place for at least 4 weeks before decorating and icing for Christmas.

christmas loaf

This is one of those recipes that, like bread and butter pudding, is great for using up spare ingredients. At Christmas, I make bread, Christmas cake and pudding, and mince pies. I collect up the odds and ends, a few ounces of the basic ingredients from them all, and make a merry Christmas loaf!

FOR THE FERMENT:
75 ml/2 fl. oz milk, warmed
15 g/½ oz fresh yeast
1 tbsp sugar
50 g/2 oz strong white flour
1 free-range egg, beaten

FOR THE DOUGH:
100 g/4 oz lard
100 g/4 oz soft brown sugar
1 free-range egg, beaten
1 tbsp black treacle
225 g/8 oz strong white flour
1 tsp salt
1 tsp baking powder
1 tsp freshly grated nutmeg
1 tbsp ground mixed spice
225 g/8 oz sultanas
100 g/4 oz currants
zest of 1 lemon, grated
zest of 1 orange, grated

For the ferment, mix all the ingredients thoroughly together in a warm bowl, cover with clingfilm and place in a warm area for 25 minutes.

To make the dough, cream the lard, sugar and egg together. Add the treacle and all the rest of the ingredients then mix them thoroughly together with the ferment.

Place the dough in a buttered loaf tin, cover with clingfilm and leave in a warm place for 40 minutes.

Preheat the oven to 200°C/400°F/Gas Mark 6.

Remove the clingfilm, place in the centre of the oven and bake for 50 to 60 minutes.

Serve with butter and jam. The wild strawberry jam on p. 220 would be perfect.

preserves

You can find some very good shop-bought marmalades and jams now but they're still never quite like home-made. When making preserves, try to use a large, heavy-based saucepan or preserving pan. Always choose firm, ripe fruit; don't use overripe fruit or the jam will not set. Gooseberries, which are plentiful in Scotland, are the only fruit which should be under-ripe for jam-making. The basic recipe for all preserves is an equal ratio of sugar to fruit. Today you can buy special jam sugar, which contains added pectin, in most supermarkets; this ensures a guaranteed, quicker setting.

Preserving jars can also be found in major supermarkets these days. I buy the ones with the rubber band and flip lids. To sterilise the jars, thoroughly wash them in hot water with a mild detergent, rinse and place on a baking tray in a very low oven (120°C/250°F/Gas Mark $\frac{1}{2}$) for 10 minutes. Remember to use oven gloves when handling the hot glasses. Even better, if you have a dishwasher, wash the jars on the glasses setting. They will come out warm, sterilised and ready to use immediately. Use a plastic funnel to fill the jars, being very careful not to burn yourself, and cover the jam with a disc of waxed or greaseproof paper. This will keep it in good condition. If you are using plastic-coated twist or screw tops, put them on as soon as the jars are filled. Label each sealed jar with the contents and date, and store in a dry, cool, dark area. Remember, damp causes mould, heat will make the contents shrink and too much light will fade their colour. All the preserves here will keep for up to 6 months, except lemon curd, which should be used within a month.

marmalade

Marmalade is one of the oldest and certainly the most famous of Scottish preserves. Whether pale gold and clear, or bronze and chunky, or anything in-between, whether made by your favourite company or at home from your favourite recipe, all varieties stem from the invention of young Janet Keiller of Dundee:

The original home of marmalade is Dundee. Its invention is accredited by long tradition to Janet Keiller (née Pierson) who married James Keiller on 1 April 1700 which is recorded in the Dundee Register.

One morning a ship from Spain, long buffeted by easterly gales, reached Tayside and deposited a cargo of oranges. Among those who gathered at the quayside was James Keiller. The oranges were going cheap and James was tempted to buy a considerable quantity; rashly, as it seemed, for owing to their bitter taste he was unable to sell them. What was to be done? His thrifty and resourceful young wife supplied the answer. We may assume that she was already skilled in the making of jams and jellies; but little could she have dreamed, as she stood over the kitchen fire, boiling and testing, that the result of her experiment would achieve world-wide renown.

The new conserve speedily caught on in Dundee, and its fame soon spread to Edinburgh. Recipes began to appear in the eighteenth-century cookbooks published in Dundee & Edinburgh, among them *The Ladies' School of Arts* by Mrs Hannah Robertson (who, incidentally, was a natural granddaughter of Charles II) and those written by Mrs Cleland and Mrs MacIver (the latter was the daughter of a Highland laird).

In 1859, a Paisley grocer and his wife, by the name of Robertson, decided to improve the flavour, which was still somewhat sharp and bitter, owing, they conjectured, to the pith and cellulose of the fruit. Together they carried out experiments until they succeeded in blending the juice and sugar into a clear jelly. Then came the crowning touch — the addition of finely shredded peel. Again Scotland, indeed Paisley, produced her famous Golden Shred marmalade.

The Scots Kitchen, F. Marian McNeill (1929)

scots orange-chip marmalade

This recipe dates from 1826 and is taken from *The Cook and Housewife's Manual* by Meg Dods.

Seville oranges, lemons, loaf sugar, water, white of egg (to clarify sugar)

Take equal weights of fine loaf sugar and Seville oranges. Wipe and grate the oranges, but not too much. (The outer grate boiled up with sugar will make an excellent conserve for rice, custard, or batter puddings.) Cut the oranges the cross way and squeeze out the juice through a small sieve. Scrape off the pulp from the inner skins and remove the seeds. Boil the skins till perfectly tender, changing the water to take off part of the bitter. When cool, scrape the coarse, white, thready part from the skins, and, trussing three or four skins together for dispatch cut them into narrow chips.

   Clarify the sugar. And put the chips, pulp, and juice to it. Add, when boiled for ten minutes, the juice and grate of two lemons to every dozen oranges.

   Skim and boil for twenty minutes; pot and cover when cold.

whisky and orange marmalade

The intensely sharp, bitter Seville oranges hold their own here, conquering the sweetness of the sugar; the fresh, intensely orange fragrance and flavour is unlike that of any other preserve anywhere in the world. Seville oranges have a very short season – late January to February – and they are the only oranges to use for a true Scots marmalade. That is why I double the quantities when I make this recipe.

Use only a really good single malt whisky like a Macallan to bring out the unique flavours of this classic marmalade; I always use the 10-year-old Macallan Fine Oak.

Remember marmalade isn't just a breakfast spread – it complements roast pork, duck or goose well.

Makes 6 x 350 ml/1 lb jars

2.25 litres/4 pt water
900 g/2 lb Seville oranges
1 lemon
1.8 kg/4 lb golden granulated sugar
220 ml/8 fl. oz single malt whisky
½ tsp butter

You will need: a preserving pan or a large, heavy-based saucepan; a 23-cm/9-in. square of muslin or gauze; some string; a funnel; and six 350 ml/1 lb jars, sterilised.

Begin by measuring the water into the pan, then cut the oranges and lemon in half and squeeze the juice out of them. Add the juice to the water, and place the pips and any bits of pith that have clung to the squeezer on the square of muslin or gauze laid over a small bowl. Now cut the orange peel into quarters with a sharp knife and then cut each quarter into thin shreds. As you cut, add the shreds to the water; any pips or spare pith you come across should be placed on the muslin. The pith contains a lot of pectin, so don't discard it. Don't worry about any pith or skin clinging to the shreds – it all gets dissolved in the boiling. Tie up the pips and pith in the muslin, forming a little bag, and tie this to the handle of the pan with the string, so that the bag is suspended in the water.

Bring the liquid to simmering point and cook gently, uncovered, for 2 hours, or until the peel is completely soft – test a piece by removing it, allowing it to cool and pressing it between your finger and thumb. At this point, pop 3 or 4 saucers into the freezer to chill.

Next, remove the bag and leave it to cool on a saucer.

Warm the sugar by stirring it in a saucepan over a low heat until the crystals are just beginning to melt. Then pour it into the pan with the orange mixture and stir it now and then over a low heat, until you can see all the crystals have melted when you test the liquid on the back of a spoon – check this carefully as it's important. Now increase the heat to very high and squeeze the muslin bag over the pan to extract all the sticky, jelly-like substance that contains the pectin. You can do this by pressing the bag between 2 saucers or by using your hands. As you squeeze, you'll see the jelly ooze out. Stir or whisk it into the rest.

As soon as the mixture reaches a fast boil, add the whisky and start timing. After 15 minutes, remove the pan from the heat, spoon a little of the marmalade onto one of the chilled saucers and pop it back in the freezer for about 20 seconds. You can tell if it is set by pushing the surface of the mixture with your finger: if it wrinkles, it is; if not, continue to boil the marmalade and give it the same test at 10-minute intervals until it does set.

After that, remove the pan from the heat. If there's a lot of scum, stir in the half teaspoon of butter. This will disperse most of it. Leave the marmalade to settle for 20 minutes and then spoon off any remaining scum.

Pour it into the hot, sterilised jars with the aid of the funnel, filling them up almost to the rims. Cover straight away with discs of greaseproof or waxed paper and seal while still hot. When cold, label and store in a dry, cool, dark place. Then hurry up and make some toast to try some!

loganberry jam

Loganberries can be picked throughout Great Britain during the summer months. They are a cross between a raspberry and a blackberry, either of which can be used for this recipe.

Makes 6 x 450 g/1 lb jars

2 kg/4 lb loganberries
2 kg/4 lb jam sugar

Place the fruit in a large saucepan and simmer gently for 10 minutes, allowing the juices to run. Add the sugar and heat gently, stirring all the time, until the sugar has dissolved. Boil rapidly for 20 minutes.

Pour into warm, sterilised jars using a plastic funnel, cover and seal.

Allow the jam to mature for at least 7 days before use.

wild strawberry jam

Wild strawberries grow all over Scotland. They are smaller and more intensely flavoured than the cultivated variety and have a longer season. They can often be purchased from the Farmers' Markets across Scotland, where they are washed and ready for use.

Makes 3 x 450 g/1 lb jars

1.4 kg/3 lb wild strawberries
1.4 kg/3 lb jam sugar
zest and juice of 1 lemon

Hull and wash the strawberries, pat them dry and cut them into quarters. Place them in a large bowl, layered with the sugar. Leave for 3 hours.

Put the contents of the bowl in a large saucepan. Add the lemon juice and zest and stir for 2 minutes, until the lemon is well mixed with the other ingredients.

Boil rapidly for 5 minutes, then turn down the heat and simmer for 15 minutes. Allow the jam to cool for 15 minutes, removing any scum using a spoon. Stir the jam to distribute the strawberries evenly, being careful not to break them up into a pulp.

Pour into warm, sterilised jars using a plastic funnel, cover and seal. Label and date the jars.

This type of jam will keep for up to 6 months.

wild rose-petal jam

Wild roses are in abundance throughout the Highlands and I last gathered my rose petals on the Isle of Lewis. I must say, once you have made this jam, you will be making it for friends and relatives all the time. Only pick the roses when they are in full blossom and ensure they are pesticide free.

Makes 3 x 450 g/1 lb jars

450 g/1 lb rose heads
900 g/2 lb jam sugar
2 litres/3⅓ pt water
juice of 4 lemons

Carefully separate the petals, snipping off any white bases. Place the petals in a large clean bowl, add half the sugar, cover with clingfilm and leave overnight in a warm place – this extracts the scent.

Pour the water and lemon juice into a large saucepan, adding the remaining sugar, heat and cook until the sugar is completely dissolved. Do not boil.

Add the rose-petal mixture, stirring all the time, then simmer gently for 30 minutes. Boil more rapidly for 3 minutes.

Pour into warm, sterilised jars using a plastic funnel, cover and seal. Leave to mature for at least 7 days before using.

lemon curd

Lemon curd has been served at lunch and tea since the early nineteenth century, not just on bread and butter but also in cheesecakes and as a filling for sponges. For a lime curd, simply replace the lemons with 6 limes.

The curd will keep for 1 month.

Makes 2 x 450 g/1 lb jars

zest and juice of 4 large lemons
225 g/8 oz butter, softened
450 g/1 lb castor sugar
5 large free-range eggs, beaten

Place the lemon juice and zest in a bowl over a saucepan of boiling water or in a double saucepan. Mix in the softened butter and sugar, whisking gently over a low heat until the sugar is completely dissolved.

Take the pan from the heat and allow it to cool for 30 seconds. Whisk in the beaten eggs. Return the pan to the heat and cook gently again for 5 to 8 minutes until the curd coats the back of a spoon.

Pour the curd into warm, sterilised jars using a plastic funnel, cover and seal.

blackcurrant and port jam

This jam is delicious with venison or with any meat you might usually accompany with cranberry sauce.

Makes 4 x 450 g/1 lb jars

1.4 kg/3 lb blackcurrants, stalks removed
1 kg/2 lb jam sugar
150 ml/⅓ pt vintage port

Put the blackcurrants in a large saucepan with the sugar and leave for 2 hours.

Simmer gently for 30 minutes until the sugar is completely dissolved. Add the port and bring to the boil. Simmer for 15 minutes, let the jam stand for 15 minutes, then boil rapidly for 5 minutes.

Pour into warm, sterilised jars using a plastic funnel, cover and seal. Allow the jam to mature for at least 14 days before use.

rowan jelly

The beautiful bright-red fruit of the rowan tree can be picked from August through to November. The rowanberries must be just ripe and the apples sweet. This is the ideal accompaniment to all game recipes.

Makes 8 x 250 g/9 oz jars

900 g/2 lb rowanberries
900 g/2 lb Cox's Orange Pippin apples
2 kg /4½ lb jam sugar

Remove any stalks from the rowanberries, wash and drain them.

Peel, core and chop the apples.

Place the fruits in a large saucepan and just cover with water. Cook for 15 minutes then strain the fruit and liquid through a fine sieve into a clean saucepan. Add the sugar. Boil rapidly for 15 minutes, until the jelly is nearly at setting point.

Pour into warm, sterilised jars using a plastic funnel, cover and seal.

piccalilli

This originated in the early twentieth century as a simple and effective way of preserving the last of the season's vegetables. You can use any crunchy vegetables which you have to hand for this recipe.

Makes 4 x 450 g/1 lb jars

200 g/7 oz small cucumbers or gherkins, cut into small dice
200 g/7 oz baby onions, peeled and cut into small dice
200 g/7 oz cauliflower florets, cut into small dice
75 g/3 oz cooking salt
600 ml/1 pt white vinegar
175 g/6 oz granulated sugar
50 g/2 oz dried English mustard powder
1 tsp turmeric
25 g/1 oz cornflour

Put the vegetables in a large dish and sprinkle with the salt. Cover and leave to stand for 24 hours.

Rinse the vegetables. In a large saucepan, heat the vinegar gently and add the vegetables.

Mix all the dry ingredients together and add to the pan, stirring. Simmer gently for 15 minutes.

Pour into warm, sterilised jars and seal with non-metallic lids. Leave for at least 2 months before using.

pickled onions

I make my pickled onions quite sweet, using a mild spiced vinegar. I find white wine vinegar less tangy than malt and the use of soft brown sugar mellows the sharpness of the pickles.

Makes 5 x 250 g/9 oz jars

FOR THE PICKLING VINEGAR:
1 litre/1¾ pt white wine or malt vinegar
8 cloves
12 g/½ oz fresh ginger
12 g/½ oz cinnamon stick
8 white peppercorns

900 g/2 lb pickling onions, peeled
100 g/4 oz soft brown sugar
12 g/½ oz salt
1 tsp pink peppercorns

To make the pickling vinegar, pour the vinegar into a clean, glass airtight container, add the other ingredients and seal. Leave for 2 months and shake the bottle every week.

For the pickled onions, put all the ingredients in a glass bowl with 600 ml/1 pt of pickling vinegar which has been warmed until it is hot but not boiling and stir with a wooden spoon until the sugar dissolves.

Pack the onions into warm, sterilised jars and top up with the vinegar, seal with non-metallic lids and leave to stand for at least 4–6 weeks.

I use the same method for pickled eggs; it is quite easy but do try to use very fresh free-range eggs. Boil a dozen slowly for 10 minutes and plunge them into cold water for at least 12 minutes. Shell the eggs, wash again and they are ready to be pickled.

pickled quails' eggs

Quails' eggs are available from major supermarkets and delicatessens, and are almost always to be found at Farmers' Markets.

Makes 4 x 150 ml/5 oz jars

2 dozen fresh quail eggs, hard boiled and shelled
600 ml/1 pt white wine vinegar
3 blades of mace

Boil the eggs for 6 minutes, stirring them after the first 2 minutes to centralise the yolks. Plunge them into cold water for 6 minutes.

Shell the eggs and pack them into warm, sterilised jars and cover with vinegar, adding a blade of mace to each jar.

Seal with non-metallic lids and leave for 1 month before using.

pickled red cabbage

Choose a really firm cabbage for this recipe. Pickled cabbage is a wonderful accompaniment to winter stews and casseroles.

Makes 4 x 250 g/9 oz jars

1 red cabbage, washed and shredded
100 g/4 oz cooking salt
50 g/2 oz soft brown sugar
600 ml/20 fl. oz white wine vinegar

Remove any discoloured leaves, cut the cabbage into quarters and cut out the inner stalk.

Place the shredded cabbage in layers with the salt and sugar in a large basin, cover with clingfilm and leave to stand for 24 hours.

Rinse the cabbage in cold water, draining it well. Pack quite loosely into warm, sterilised jars, cover with the vinegar and seal with non-metallic lids.

Let the red cabbage stand for at least 7 days before using. It should be eaten within 3 months or it will lose its crispness.

beetroot and rhubarb chutney

This is an exciting taste of the Scottish hills, perfect with game. Brian Olverson's family has been growing beetroot for centuries and their fresh Red Velvet beetroot is sold by Marks and Spencer. This recipe is for Brian.

Makes 5 x 250 g/9 oz jars

450 g/1 lb cooked beetroot, diced
450 g/1 lb rhubarb, washed and chopped
2 onions, chopped
3 tbsp sultanas
1 tbsp green peppercorns in brine
4 tbsp soft brown sugar
pinch cayenne pepper
1 tsp salt
1 tbsp mild curry paste
2 tbsp port
150 ml/⅓ pt white wine vinegar

Put all the ingredients into a large saucepan, bring to the boil and simmer slowly for 10 minutes, stirring all the time. Let the mixture stand for 30 minutes. Bring back to the boil and simmer for 30 minutes.

Pour into warm, sterilised jars, cover and seal with non-metallic lids. Allow to mature for 3 weeks before using.

wild strawberry vinegar

This is a tasty summer vinegar for pouring over baby beetroot or blending with a little olive oil and Arran mustard for a salad dressing.

Makes 3 x 275 ml/$\frac{1}{2}$ pt bottles

900 g/2 lb wild strawberries
2 litres/3⅓ pt white wine vinegar
900 g/2 lb granulated sugar

Put the hulled strawberries in a large, clean glass bowl. Pour over enough vinegar to cover the strawberries. Cover with clingfilm and leave to stand for 4 days, stirring every day.

Strain the liquid through a non-metallic sieve, being very careful not to crush the strawberries through the sieve as this will make the vinegar cloudy. Pour the juices into a saucepan, add the sugar, bring to the boil and simmer for 20 minutes.

Let the liquid stand until it is completely cold and then bottle using cork or plastic stoppers. Leave to stand for at least 4 days before use.

appendix –
ode to the haggis

25 January, the anniversary of Burns' birth in 1759, is the night to toast the haggis. I get so many people turning their noses up at this classic dish. I always say, 'Don't knock it until you've tried it.' The ingredients of haggis vary but essentially it consists of lamb, lamb's heart and liver, oatmeal, onion and spices.

The very first Burns Supper took place on 21 July 1801, five years after Robert Burns died, at the cottage in Alloway where he was born. (It has now been restored and is well worth a visit.) A few of the poet's well-loved friends and cronies gathered to share a simple meal and a dram or two, and to fondly remember the life and genius of Scotland's national poet.

Over the last 200 years, that simple meal has grown to become a celebration of Robert Burns held throughout the world, from Tokyo to Tallahassee. Not just Scots but people from every race and creed delight in the memory of a poet who championed the brotherhood of man and defended the value of humour and comradeship against hypocrisy and prejudice.

Even Queen Victoria toasted and tasted the haggis while dining at Blair Castle, the home of the Duke and Duchess of Atholl. The Queen recorded in her journal: 'There were several Scotch dishes, two soups and the celebrated "Haggis", which I tried last night and really liked very much. The Duchess was delighted with my taking it.'

So how do you serve haggis? Contrary to popular belief, haggis, like black pudding, is already cooked and needs only to be reheated. I like to reheat mine by steaming it but you can use whichever method you prefer: steaming, boiling, baking or microwaving. Mind you, Rabbie Burns might turn in his grave if you did microwave it!

Personally, I like haggis with its traditional accompaniments – neeps and tatties – served with a wee dram of Macallan whisky. I also use haggis as a stuffing for chicken, duck, goose and game birds.

THE SELKIRK GRACE
Some hae meat and canna eat
And some wad eat that want it;
But we hae meat and we can eat
Sae let the Lord be thankit
Anon., often attributed to Burns

a typical burns supper programme

Grace

Following their arrival and reception by the chairman, guests are called to the table and offer an opening grace, traditionally the Selkirk Grace.

The grace is followed by a good warming soup such as my cullen skink (see p. 31) or cock-a-leekie (see p. 33).

Haggis

The haggis is paraded into the hall, led by a piper playing a traditional tune.

The haggis is laid before the chairman whereupon a designated speaker recites Burns' 'To a Haggis'.

After a whisky is offered to chef, piper and speaker, the haggis is ceremonially sliced and served with chappit neeps and tatties (mashed turnips and potatoes).

There then follow as many courses of good Scots food, accompanied by plenty of whisky or Scots ale, as is deemed fitting, finished off with a dessert such as clootie dumpling (see p. 182) or cranachan (see p. 170), again served with a dram of whisky.

The Immortal Memory

Either the chairman or a guest speaker delivers the Immortal Memory address, which remembers the life and work of Robert Burns and often addresses an aspect that has some relevance to the present day or to the assembled company. At the end, the speaker invites guests to stand and toast the immortal memory of the Bard of Ayr.

Toast to the Lassies

A speaker offers a light-hearted and often irreverent tribute to the women present, often illustrated by quotations from Burns.

Reply from the Lassies

On behalf of the lassies, a speaker will often demonstrate that the fairer sex has the sharper tongue.

Tam O'Shanter

For many, the highlight of the evening. A star speaker recites Burns' best-loved poem, telling the cautionary tale of what befell poor Tam, a 'blethering, blustering, drunken blellum', when he ignored his good wife's advice.

Music, Songs and Poems

As the chairman determines, the evening may proceed with Scots music, readings and/or dancing as the mood befits.

Closing Remarks

The Chairman closes the evening with a warm thanks to the assembled company and often a more formal vote of thanks to those who have helped the evening go so well. Finally, to cap off an unmatchable evening, all guests join in singing Burns' most famous, and the world's favourite, song, 'Auld Lang Syne'.

to a haggis

Fair fa' your honest, sonsie face,
Great Chieftan o' the Puddin-race!
Aboon them a' ye tak your place,
Painch, tripe, or thairm:
Weel are ye wordy o' a grace
As lang's my arm.

The groaning trencher there ye fill,
Your hurdies like a distant hill,
Your pin wad help to mend a mill
In time o' need,
While thro' your pores the dews distil
Like amber bead.

His knife see Rustic-labour dight,
An' cut you up wi' ready sleight,
Trenching your gushing entrails bright

Like onie ditch;
And then, O what a glorious sight,
Warm-reekin, rich!

Then, horn for horn they stretch an' strive,
Deil tak the hindmost, on they drive,
Till a' their weel-swall'd kytes belyve
Are bent like drums;
Then auld Guidman, maist like to rive,
'Bethankit' hums.

Is there that owre his French *ragout*,
Or *olio* that wad staw a sow,
Or *fricassee* wad mak her spew
Wi' perfect sconner,
Looks down wi' sneering, scornfu' view
On sic a dinner?

Poor devil! see him owre his trash,
As feckless as a wither'd rash,
His spindle shank a guid whip-lash,
His nieve a nit;
Thro' bluidy flood or field to dash,
O how unfit!

But mark the Rustic, haggis-fed,
The trembling earth resounds his tread;
Clap in his walie nieve a blade,
He'll mak it whissle;
An' legs, an' arms, an' heads will sned
Like taps o' thrissle.

Ye Pow'rs wha mak mankind your care,
And dish them out their bill o' fare,
Auld Scotland wants nae skinking ware
That jaups in luggies;
But if you wish her gratefu' prayer,
Gie her a Haggis!

Robert Burns, 1786

recommended suppliers

ANDY RACE FISH MERCHANTS

The Harbour
Mallaig
Inverness-shire
PH41 4PX
Tel: 01687 462 626
Fax: 01687 462 060
Email: sales@andyrace.co.uk
www.andyrace.co.uk
Known by chefs throughout Britain for the quality of their seafood. The *Sunday Telegraph Magazine* said of their smoked salmon: 'A real treat, peat perfect'. I second that.

ARDTARAIG FINE FOODS

Riverslea
Tarholm
Annbank
Ayr
KA6 5HX
Tel: 01292 521 000
Fax: 01292 521 021
Email: info@ardtaraigfinefoods.co.uk
www.ardtaraigfinefoods.co.uk
Ardtaraig specialise in gift hampers. You must try their smoked oysters.

BROUGH BUTCHERS

10 Burscough Street
Ormskirk
Lancashire
L39 2ER
Tel: 01695 579 520
Email: mark@broughs.com
www.broughs.com
Suppliers of Aberdeen Angus beef in the north-west of England.

CLUNY FISH SUPPLIES

1-3 Low Street
Buckie
Moray
AB56 1UX
Tel: 01542 833 950
Fax: 01542 835 950
Email: clunyfish@lineone.net
www.clunyfish.co.uk
I buy my smoked king scallops from
Cluny's.

THE CROSS GAITS INN

Beverley Road
Blacko
Nelson
Lancashire
BB9 6RF
Tel: 01282 616 312
The source of the rabbit recipe on p. 78,
Peter Smith of the Cross Gaits is renowned
for using the finest Scottish ingredients.

DAMHEAD ORGANIC FOODS

32a Damhead
Old Pentland Road
Lothianburn
Edinburgh
EH10 7EA
Tel: 0131 448 2091
Fax: 0131 448 2113
Email: enquiries@damhead.co.uk
www.damhead.co.uk
Everything organic for those who love
eating healthily.

DE VERE CAMERON HOUSE HOTEL

Loch Lomond
Dunbartonshire
G83 8QZ
Tel: 01389 755 565
Fax: 01389 759 522
Email: reservations@cameronhouse.co.uk
www.devereonline.co.uk

DEANHEAD DAIRY

North Road
Burnside
Inverkeithing
Fife
KY11 1HQ
Tel: 01383 412 586
Fax: 01383 410 440

DONALD RUSSELL DIRECT

Harlaw Road
Inverurie
Aberdeenshire
AB51 4FR
Tel: 01467 629 666
Fax: 01467 629 434
Email: info@donaldrussell.co.uk
www.donaldrusselldirect.com
Mail order at its very best – a fantastic
range of award-winning meat cut to a
kitchen-ready standard.

DUNKELD SMOKED SALMON

Springwells Smokehouse
Brae Street
Dunkeld
Perthshire
PH8 0BA
Tel: 01350 727 639
Fax: 01350 728 760
Email: enquiries@dunkeldsmokedsalmon.com
www.dunkeldsmokedsalmon.com
Traditionally cured smoked salmon, from the banks of the Tay to your door.

FLETCHERS OF AUCHTERMUCHTY

Reediehill Deer Farm
Auchtermuchty
Fife
KY14 7HS
Tel: 01337 828 369
Fax: 01337 827 001
Email: info@fletcherscotland.co.uk
www.seriouslygoodvenison.co.uk
Speaks for itself – seriously good venison in every cut you could require.

HARVEY NICHOLS

30–34 St Andrews Square
Edinburgh
EH2 2AD
Tel: 0131 524 8388
Fax: 0131 524 8317
Email: contactedinburgh@harveynichols.com
www.harveynichols.com
Harvey Nicks' only Scottish store has a fantastic food hall with a great selection, including many of the Scottish specialities mentioned in the book.

HEBRIDEAN SMOKEHOUSE

Clachan
Locheport
North Uist
HS6 5HD
Tel: 01876 580 209
Fax: 01876 580 323
Email: sales@hebrideansmokehouse.com
www.hebrideansmokehouse.com
Hebridean use peat to smoke their trout and salmon, giving it a really special flavour.

ISLAY FINE FOOD COMPANY LTD

Rockside Farm
Bruichladdich
Isle of Islay
PA49 7UT
Tel: 01496 850 350
Fax: 01496 850 209
Email: info@islayfinefood.com
www.islayfinefood.com
Mark and Rohaise French make the finest smoked beef, lamb and venison, which is thinly sliced and tastes divine. I love their Islay Smoked Beef with Malt Whisky, which is great in a salad.

ISLE OF ARRAN DISTILLERS

Visitor Centre
Lochranza
Arran
KA27 8HJ
Tel: 01770 830 264
Fax: 01770 830 364
Email: arran.distillers@arranwhisky.com
www.arranwhisky.com
Home of Robert Burns Malt Whisky –
perfect for a Burns supper!

ISLE OF SKYE SEAFOOD

Broadford
Skye
IV49 9AP
Tel: 01471 822 135
Fax: 01471 822 166
Email: sales@skye-seafood.co.uk
www.skye-seafoods.co.uk
Locally caught, fresh seafood including
lobster, crab, mussels and scallops.

JAMESFIELD ORGANIC CENTRE

Jamesfield Farm
Abernethy
Fife
KY14 6EW
Tel: 01738 850 498
Fax: 01738 850 741
Email: jamesfieldfarm@btconnect.com
www.jamesfieldfarm.com
Ian Miller and his brother Roy sell meat
and vegetables from their organic farm.
Their website also includes an online
organic grocery store.

JENNERS EDINBURGH

48 Princes Street
Edinburgh
EH2 2YJ
Tel: 0131 225 2248
Fax: 0131 260 2240
www.jenners.com
I cannot recommend Jenners highly
enough – a great selection of Scottish
specialities in a great setting, whether it's
Edinburgh or Loch Lomond.

JENNERS LOCH LOMOND SHORES

Ben Lomond Way
Balloch
Dunbartonshire
G83 8QL
Tel: 01389 722 200

JUDITH GLUE ORKNEY HAMPERS

25 Broad Street
Kirkwall
Orkney
KW15 1DH
Tel: 01856 874 225
Fax: 01856 876 263
Email: info@judithglue.com
www.judithglue.com
A selection of hampers featuring local
produce. Judith's choices are excellent.

KINGDOM SEAFOOD

23 East Shore
Pittenweem
Fife
KY10 2NH
Tel: 01333 311 263
Fax: 01333 312 182
Email: admin@kingdomseafood.co.uk
www.kingdomseafood.co.uk
Where the fishing fleet of the picturesque
East Neuk of Fife sell their catch. Great for
langoustines and salmon.

LINDSAY GRIEVE

29 High Street
Hawick
TD9 9BU
Tel: 01450 372 109
Email: info@angus.co.uk
www.angus.co.uk/haggis/
Award-winning haggis from the Borders.

THE LIVING ROOM

113–115 George Street
Edinburgh
EH2 4JN
Tel: 08704 422 718
Email: edinburgh@thelivingroom.co.uk
www.thelivingroom.co.uk

LOCH FYNE OYSTERS LTD

Clachan
Cairndow
Argyll
PA26 8BL
Tel: 01499 600 264
Fax: 01499 600 234
Email: info@lochfyne.com
www.lochfyne.com

Here are the Loch Fyne restaurant
locations and phone numbers for your
perusal. Spoil yourself with some fresh
oysters and a glass of chilled champagne.

Barnet: 020 8449 3674
Bath: 01225 750 120
Beaconsfield: 01494 679 960
Brighton: 01273 716 160
Bristol: 0117 930 7160
Cambridge: 01223 362 433
Cairndow: 01499 600 236
Covent Garden: 020 7240 4999
Elton: 01832 280 298
Fulham Road: 020 7610 8020
Guildford: 01483 230 550
Harrogate: 01423 533 070
Henley: 01491 845 780
Knowle: 01564 732 750
Loughton: 020 8532 5140
Norwich: 01603 723 450
Nottingham: 0115 988 6840
Ogham: 01784 414 890
Oxford: 01865 292 510
Portsmouth: 02392 778 060
Reading: 0118 918 5850
Sevenoaks: 01732 467 140
Nottingham: 01159 886 840
Twickenham: 020 8255 6222
Winchester: 01962 872 930

THE MACALLAN

Visitor Centre
Easter Elchies
Craigellachie
AB38 9RX
Tel: 01340 872 280
www.themacallan.com
When I talk about whisky, this is the one I mean!

MACBETH'S OF FORRES

11 Tolbooth Street
Forres
Morayshire
IV36 1PH
Tel/Fax: 01309 672 254
Email: enquiries@macbeths.com
www.macbeths.com
I have been buying from this company since 1986 and I have used every product, from rabbit, guinea fowl and pigeon to venison and beef – you name it, Michael and Susan Gibson have it.

MACSWEEN OF EDINBURGH

Dryden Road
Bilston Glen
Loanhead
Edinburgh
EH20 9LZ
Tel: 0131 440 2555
Fax: 0131 440 2674
Email: haggis@macsween.co.uk
www.macsween.co.uk
Renowned haggis specialists who also make a delicious vegetarian version.

MOIDART SMOKEHOUSE

Dalnabreac
Acharacle
Argyll
PH36 4JX
Tel/Fax: 01967 431 214
Email: info@moidartsmokehouse.co.uk
www.moidartsmokehouse.co.uk
Oak-smoked salmon, trout and chicken.

NORMAN OLVERSON LTD

Red Velvet Beetroot
Smithy Lane
Kershaw's Farm
Scarisbrick
near Ormskirk
Lancashire
L40 8HN
Tel: 01704 840 392
Fax: 01704 841 096
Email: info@redvelvet.co.uk
www.redvelvet.co.uk
The best beetroot, grown in black-soil country. Recommended for my beetroot chutney (see p. 227).

THE ORKNEY CHEESE COMPANY

Crowness Road
Hatston
Kirkwall
Orkney
KW15 1RG
Tel: 01856 872 824
Fax: 01856 872 402
Email: info@orkneycheese.com
www.orkneycheese.com

THE ORKNEY HERRING COMPANY

Garson Food Park
Stromness
Orkney
KW16 3JU
Tel: 01856 850 514
Fax: 01856 850 568
Email: ken@orkneyherring.com

ORKNEY MEAT

Grainshore Road
Hatston
Kirkwall
Orkney
KW15 1FL
Tel: 01856 874 326
Fax: 01856 872 496
Email: info@orkneymeat.co.uk
www.orkneymeat.co.uk
Home of Orkney Gold, tender beef,
matured for a minimum of ten days.

ORKNEY ORGANIC MEAT

New Holland Farm
Holm
Orkney
KW17 2SA
Tel/Fax: 01856 781 345
Email: info@orkneyorganicmeat.co.uk
www.orkneyorganicmeat.co.uk
Organic Aberdeen Angus beef and grass-
fed lamb.

ORKNEY WINE COMPANY

Operahalla
St Ola
Kirkwall
Orkney
KW15 1SX
Tel: 01856 878 700
Fax: 01856 878 701
Email: info@orkneywine.co.uk
www.orkneywine.co.uk

PETRIE FINE FOODS

West Langton Farm
Dunlop
Ayrshire
KA3 4BL
Tel: 01560 484 861
Fax: 01560 485 858
Email: petriefinefoods@btinternet.com
www.alchemedia.co.uk/petrie/
Traditional Christmas puddings and
whisky cakes.

RAMSAY OF CARLUKE

22 Mount Stewart Street
Carluke
South Lanarkshire
ML8 5ED
Tel: 01555 772 277
Fax: 01555 750 686
Email: websales@ramsayofcarluke.co.uk
www.ramsayofcarluke.co.uk.

RANNOCH SMOKERY

Kinloch Rannoch
by Pitlochry
Perthshire
PH16 5QD
Tel: 0870 160 1559
Fax: 0870 160 1558
Email: enquires@rannochsmokery.co.uk
www.rannochsmokery.co.uk
Wonderful smoked meats and fish,
including venison, duck and pheasant.

SALAR SMOKEHOUSE LTD

The Pier
Lochcarnan
South Uist
HS8 5PD
Tel: 01870 610 324
Fax: 01870 610 369
Email: sales@salar.co.uk
www.salar.co.uk

SCOTTISHORGANICLAMB.COM

Knockreoch
Dalry
Castle Douglas
DG7 3XS
Tel/Fax: 01644 430 354
Email: enquiries@scottishorganiclamb.com
www.scottishorganiclamb.com
One of my favourite companies – their
convenient service will provide you with
vacuum-packed cuts of the finest naturally
reared lamb.

STAG'S BREATH LIQUEUR

Meikles of Scotland
Station Road
Newtonmore
PH20 1AR
Tel: 01540 673 733
Fax: 01540 673 614
Email: info@stagsbreath.co.uk
www.stagsbreath.co.uk
A liqueur made from whisky and comb
honey. Have a look at their website to see
how the name came about – the story is
fascinating.

TEVIOT GAME FARE SMOKERY

Teviot Water Gardens
Kirkbank House
Kelso
TD5 8LE
Tel: 01835 850 253
Fax: 01835 850 293
Email: teviot.gamefare@btconnect.com
www.teviotgamefaresmokery.co.uk
Smoked fish, game are available by mail
order, but the smokery is well worth a
visit. Set in beautiful water gardens, it has
an excellent restaurant and also runs a
smoking service for anglers and hunters.

TILQUHILLIE PUDDINGS

Maryfield Farm
Banchory
Kincardineshire
AB31 6HY
Tel/Fax: 01330 822 037
Email: tillqpudds@tiscali.co.uk
www.strathdee.com/tilquhillie
The finest sweet puddings and clootie dumplings. Tilquhillie specialise in wheat-free puddings made with oats and suitable for many allergy sufferers.

TOBERMORY FISH COMPANY

Main Street
Tobermory
Mull
PA75 6NU
Tel: 01688 302 120
Fax: 01688 302 622
Email: sales@tobermoryfish.co.uk
www.tobermoryfish.co.uk
Susie Carmichael sells the fabulous smoked mussels and natural finnan haddock.

bibliography

Acton, Eliza, *Modern Cookery in all its branches*, 1845, Longman, Brown, Green and Longmans

Beeton, Isabella, *The Book of Household Management*, 1861, S.O. Beeton

Bridge, Tom, *The Golden Age of Cookery*, 1983, Ross Anderson

Bridge, Tom, *200 Classic Sauces*, 1995, Cassell

Bridge, Tom, *Bridge over Britain*, 1996, Cassell

Bridge, Tom, *Bridge on British Beef*, 1997, Piatkus

Bridge, Tom, *Chicken* (What's Cooking series), 2000, Paragon

Bridge, Tom, *The Golden Age of Food*, 1999, Waterton

Bridge, Tom, *The Ultimate Game Cookbook*, 1999, Piatkus

Dods, Margaret, *The Cook and Housewife's Manual*, 1826, Beaumont and Fletcher

Francatelli, Charles Elme, *The Cook's Guide*, 1869, Richard Bentley

Glasse, Hannah, *The Art of Cookery Made Plain and Easy*, 1747

Graig, Elizabeth, *New Standard Cookery*, 1932, Odhams Press

Heath, Ambose, *The Good Breakfast Cookbook*, 1945, Faber & Faber

Jewry, Mary, *Warne's Model Cookery and Housekeeping Book*, 1868, Fredrick Warne

Kitchiner, Dr William, *The Cook's Oracle*, 1817, J. Moyes

Marshall, Agnes. B, *Mrs A.B. Marshall's Cookery Book*, 1888, Simkin & Marshall

McNeill, Marian, *The Scots Kitchen*, 1929, Blackie

Pegge, Samuel, *A Forme of Cury*, 1780, J. Nicholls

Raffald, Elizabeth, *The Experienced English House-keeper*, 1769, J. Harrop

The Young Woman's Companion or Frugal Housewife, 1811, Russell and Allen

acknowledgements

Writing this book is one of the most enjoyable tasks I have ever undertaken. Why? Because there is no other place in the world like Scotland. The people are the friendliest I have ever come across and many could learn a great deal from their hospitality. It was not a hardship writing this book, but a complete and utter joy working with the numerous people involved. I have tried to make this book a very honest and back-to-basics book on the finest of Scottish food and drink, and with that in mind I owe a great deal of thanks to the people of Scotland and a very special book and its author Christina Jane Johnstone. She wrote *The Cook and Housewife's Manual* in 1826 under the pseudonym Meg Dods.

My first big thank you is to Dr Tim Pigott and all the staff at The Walton Centre for Neurology and Neurosurgery in Liverpool for bringing me back to full health. Without them I would not be here today.

Acknowledgement and huge thank yous go to the following: Hubert and Carol Lowry for being very dear friends to me and my wife, Jayne; J.E.B. for giving me Lodge 88 at Cameron House and Gaynor Black for introducing me to Cameron House; Shona Brierton, sales and marketing manager; Joe Longmuir, general manager; and that unique executive chef Simon Whitley for the fantastic food and hospitality at the De Vere Cameron House. If you have never been, please take my advice and visit, not just for the food but also for the hospitality and stunning views of Loch Lomond.

Thanks again to Shona for introducing me to Noelle Campbell, the public relations and marketing officer for Argyll, the Isles, Loch Lomond, Stirling and the Trossachs Tourist Board in Stirling.

I am grateful to Jeff Bland, executive chef at the Balmoral Hotel and Number One restaurant in Edinburgh and to Emma Offord for all her hard work with regards to persuading Jeff to come up with a fantastic classic recipe for the book. This year, Number One retained its Michelin star and in April the Balmoral was named Hotel of the Year by HotelReviewScotland.com – another fantastic accolade for everyone there.

Thanks are also due to Andrew Cameron of Scottish Food and Drink at the Food Information Executive; John Clarke from Orkney Marketing Services; *The Orcadian* for permission to quote from Alan Bichan's article on clapshot; Virginia Sumsion, marketing manager, Loch Fyne Oysters Ltd; my dear friend John Fallon of Grants Foods (especially for providing information and material on Burns Suppers) and Angela Pollock, his technical manager, for all her help in development of products; Stephen Hallam, managing director at Dickinson & Morris in Melton Mowbray; the directors and staff at Jenners, Edinburgh; and Gillian Rogers and her very helpful staff at Jenners at Loch Lomond Shores in Balloch. It's well worth a visit to see the vast array of Scottish food and drink, especially the unrivalled 'whisky wall'.

Thanks also to chef Stuart Muir and Deanna Williams, the foodmarket manager, at Harvey Nichols, St Andrew Square, Edinburgh; Alexandra Fitch and Sharon McLaughlin at the Edrington Group, the home of Macallan, for the finest whisky in the world; Tim Bacon, John Branagan, Rob Bastow, and everyone at Living Ventures and the Living Room restaurants in George Street, Edinburgh, and St Vincent Street, Glasgow; Richard Russum for making a marvellous job of my chef's whites, for catering equipment and for offering to stock this book – after all, Russums (www.russums.co.uk) are the UK's largest dedicated online culinary book retailer.

I am grateful, too, to the Orkney Cheese Company; Nigel Murray at Klinge Foods, makers of LoSalt, the only salt that is good for the heart; Jill and Bill Adron for putting the O factor into oats at Tilquhillie Puddings in Banchory; Peter Smith and his beautiful daughter Hannah; and Helen Atkinson for looking after me on my every visit to the Cross Gaits at Blacko near Nelson; my favourite hotelier, Dee Ludlow, for being a good friend – I will be creating recipes from this book at Hintlesham Hall in Suffolk very soon, Dee.

Thanks to Nishita Assomull from Wild Card for the food photographs and PR advice with regards to Donald Russell Meats; John, Andrew and Jacqueline, the Ramsay family from Carluke, who have been curing Ayrshire bacon, making pork products and producing black pudding since 1857; Michael and Susan Gibson, the managing directors of one of the finest meat and game companies in Scotland, Macbeths of Forres; Emile and Marjolein van Schayk from the Orkney Wine

Company in Kirkwall, Orkney, for letting me sample the most beautiful of Scottish wines; Jane Fenton for her beautiful photographs; finally, Becky Pickard, Claire Rose, Graeme Blaikie and Bill Campbell at Mainstream Publishing, Edinburgh, for having faith in me and helping to complete this book.

Aye
Tom Bridge

index

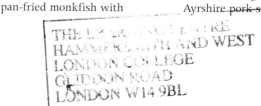